PICTON'S PRICED CATALOGUE AND HANDBOOK OF PICTORIAL POSTCARDS AND THEIR POSTMARKS 1983

Ron Mead Joan Venman
Dr J. T. Whitney

D1350680

LONGMAN
London and New York

Longman Group Limited,
Longman House,
Burnt Mill, Harlow, Essex UK

Published in the United States of America by Longman Inc., New York

© BPH Publications 1971 (two editions), 1973, 1976 (two editions), 1977, 1979 (two editions),
1980, 1981
© BPH Publications and R. Mead, J. Venman and Dr J. T. Whitney 1982

First published in UK 1971 by BPH Publications
Second edition 1971
Third edition 1973
Fourth edition 1976
Fifth edition 1977
Sixth edition 1979
Seventh edition 1979
Eighth edition 1980
Ninth edition 1981
Tenth edition published in UK 1982 by Longman Group Limited

British Library Cataloguing in Publication Data
Picton's priced postcard catalogue and handbook.—
    1983
    1. Postal cards—Great Britain—Catalogs—
    Periodicals
    769.56'6   NC1872
ISBN 0 582 50320 5

Library of Congress Cataloging in Publication Data
Mead, Ron.
    Picton's priced catalogue and handbook of pictorial postcards and their postmarks, 1983.
    Rev. ed. of: Picton's priced catalogue of British pictorial postcards and postmarks,
1894–1939/M. R. Hewlett. 4th Ed. 1976.
    Bibliography: p.
    Includes index.
    1. Postmarks—Great Britain—Catalogs.
    2. Postal cards—Great Britain—Catalogs. I. Venman, Joan. II. Whitney, J. T. III. Hewlett,
M. R. (Maurice Raymond). Picton's priced catalogue of British pictorial postcards and
postmarks, 1894–1939. IV. Title.
HE6184.C3M4 1982   769.56'6   82–6579
ISBN 0 582 50320 5   AACR2

Typeset by Chippenham Typesetting, Chippenham.
Printed in Great Britain by Picton Print,
Citadel Works, Bath Road, Chippenham, Wilts SN15 2AB.
Paper Supplied by Howard Smith Papers, Bristol.

CONTENTS

PREFACE

One of the most encouraging signs of 1982 has been the formation of many more postcard clubs including several devoted to specialist studies.

As we reported last year, there appears to be no sign of recession in postcards, with provincial events particularly standing up well, with the number of dealers, attendance and total spent at last year's British International Exhibition (BIPEX) all improving. The only cloud visible being the lack of good quality material, both topographical and subject, as mentioned last year. This must surely be the only hobby where members of the trade continuously moan about not being able to spend their money!

We think that 1983 will be the year of the 'overseas' postcard, the demand coming both from philatelic sources and from those countries which have a strong collecting tradition.

Because this catalogue is now being published by Longman International, it will be distributed world-wide and therefore will open up the hobby to more collectors.

Old-age pensions were introduced in U.K. on 1st Jan 1909. This card used on 14th in Bognor £12

NOTES ON THE PRICES
SHOWN IN THIS CATALOGUE

Where in the pricing, a high and low figure are quoted, the reader must use his own judgement and decide where the specimen under consideration lies. There is no *rigid price control* on postcards. It is in the eye of the beholder and maybe London and some of the larger conurbations are accustomed to higher prices than those ruling in the more rural areas and isolated towns. The reader must grade such cards for himself, but this catalogue does indicate whether a card is common, medium valued or a rarity, according to the prices shown.

Condition is very important

Prices in the catalogue are for subject cards in *perfect*, and topographical cards in *acceptable*, condition.

If a mint (unused) card has a defect then the price can be reduced at once and if the defect is really serious the card becomes valueless. With used (usually stamped and cancelled) cards if the writing or postal markings are unsightly further reductions in price have to be made. Remember that a glossy transparent 'bag' covers a multitude of sins so take the card out before buying!

Many postcards are illustrated by an artist whose name appears somewhere on the card. In many cases it will be found that the 'value of the artist' exceeds that of the value of the classification. Users of the catalogue should therefore check the artist section before finally pricing a card. To a lesser degree certain photographers/publishers/printers are so popular that the price for that aspect often exceeds that of the theme price so that a quick consideration of 'maker' is also necessary before finally pricing a card.

Procedure for Pricing

An *unused card*, i.e. with no writing or adhesive stamp upon it at all, is much easier to price than a used one with an adhesive stamp. With unused cards if there is no artist or publisher to consider then just look for the appropriate classification in the index. If the card is *used*, then having decided its value had is been *unused*, one has another aspect to consider. Is the postmark of greater value than the classification?

Some people read the writing on their used cards and at times the information thereon over-rides all the previous valuation possibilities. Sometimes the signature is a valuable autograph.

To settle a vexed question about pricing one cannot add up all the valuations arising from the above facets of pricing. Normally the highest factor of pricing should be taken with maybe a little 'rounding up' if other valuable factors co-exist.

Cards produced after 1939
Obviously they lack 'age' but how long will it take for picture postcards of all classifications of such 'later vintages' to acquire a premium over their normal shop sale price for use in correspondence? Here is where the younger collectors can use their perspicacity to seek out those 'modern' cards which are going to appreciate in the long term.

GLOSSARY

APPLIQUÉ Postcards to which some 'material' has been attached are termed 'applique'. It may take the form of cloth to adorn part of the picture or a small piece of metal like a medal, or even human hair.

COMPOSITES Where a number of postcards are required in order to make up a large picture, the set of such cards is referred to as a composite set. They were usually issued in sets of between three to twelve cards.

DIVIDED BACKS (see Undivided Backs)

EMBOSSED These have part of the surface of the card pressed upwards and are found for example on heraldic subjects and many greetings cards.

ETHNIC These refer to postcards depicting the indigenous race(s) of any country in their characteristic costumes and/or activities.

FABS These are cards which have upon them a square of silk with a printed design which could be removed and used for patchwork decoration. The cards are adverts for Sharpe's of Bradford.

GRUSS AUS This is German for 'Greetings from' and to some extent was the originating idea for pictorial postcards, i.e. folks away from home sent such cards to their friends and relations to indicate where they were staying. This is a very popular Continental classification.

HOLD TO LIGHT (H.T.L. abbreviation) These are all cards which you look through against some form of light. There are three types:
(a) **Cut outs**. The construction of the card is such that coloured (yellow or blue are very popular) translucent material is introduced to cover the 'cut out sections' so that on holding to light, the cut out sections, being transparent, allow the light through, hence their name – transparencies. The cards are usually thicker than normal. They often depict 'windows' at night with 'light' shining therefrom.
(b) **Colour changes** or **chameleons**. On holding to the light, the *colours of the* **same** *picture*, as the name suggests, change, usually for the better, because the normal appearance of the card is drab.
(c) **Scene changes** or **metamorphics**. These are the rarest of the H.T.L.s. On holding them to the light a *different* scene appears.

The instruction 'Hold to Light' is often printed in an oblong box on the picture side in: French – Carte Transparente; German – Bitte Gegen Das Licht Zu Halten; English – Pray hold this card up to the light, and you shall see a charming sight.

MAGIC CARDS These reveal a picture when heat or friction or a chemical is applied to them.

MONTAGE These are postcards depicting persons or scenes composed of postage stamps, etc., cut up and pasted upon the card to produce the picture involved. Chinese stamps seem the most commonly used and then Japanese. Much time must have been spent in producing them.

OFFICIALS Cards issued by an authority, such as a Railway or Shipping Company, primarily for use as stationery or advertising.

PANEL CARDS These are postcards produced on very thick card.

PATRIOTICS These usually carry the flag or emblem of the country concerned with some national event or characteristic indicated. Highly popular cards, usually coloured.

PULL OUTS Where strips of views, etc. are folded under flaps on the face of the cards and 'pulled out' to view.

REWARD CARDS The London County Council Education Department used to issue postcards to pupils who excelled in various aspects of scholastic life. Other Education Authorities have issued them, as well as other types of organisations.

TINSEL (or GLITTER) Many cards bear this minor embellishment, i.e. best described as a minor metallic application which glistens. It is the most common form of adornment.

UNDIVIDED BACKS When postcards using adhesive stamps were first allowed in 1894, the back, in postcard collectors' parlance, was reserved exclusively for the address and the adhesive stamp, i.e. no message was permitted on the back. The message if any had to be on the picture side so the picture did not fill the whole of the front, but consisted of a vignette and space for the message. Undivided backs persisted until late in 1902, although Regulations permitted the divided back to be used in 1897.

VIGNETTE A small picture on the front of a postcard, usually found on cards with undiveded backs. A message could be written on the space left.

WRITE AWAY A pictorial card bearing the opening phrase of a sentence which required completion by the sender. Very popular in Edwardian Days as holiday correspondents seemed 'at a loss for words' and this type of card made life easy for them.

Becoming very popular A. H. Fullwood's Australasian views £3

ARTISTS

The artists listed in this section will also be found cross referenced under subject headings where appropriate. **General artists are listed here only.**

A.E.	Comic	75
Abeille, Jack	Glamour	£20
Acker, Flori von	General	40
Ackroyd, W.M.	Animals	£1.50
Adams, M.	General	40
Adams, Will	Comic	£1.50
Addison, W.G.	General	40
Ainsley, Anne	Animals	50
Albertini	Glamour	£2
Aldin, Cecil	Animals	£3
Allan, A.	General	40
Allen, S.J.	General	40
Alys, M.	Children	£1
Ambler, C.	Animals	50
Anders, O.	Animals	£2+
	Comic	£2
Anderson, V.C.	Children	£1
Aris, Ernest	Comic	£2
Armitage, A.	General	50
Asti, Angelo	Glamour	£1.50
Attwell, Mabel Lucie	Children	
	Early	£2
	Middle	£1.50
	Later	£1
	Mod Repros	20–40
Austerlitz, E.	Comic	£2.50
Austin, E.H.S. Barnes-	Animals	£4
Austin, Winifred	Birds	75
Aveling, S.	General	£1.50
Azzoni, A.	Children	£1
Bairnsfather, Bruce	Comic/Military	£1.50
Baker, H. Granville	Military	£3
Ball, Wilfred	General	50
Balestrieri, L.	Glam/Gen	£5
Bamber, George A.	Comic	75
Barber, C.W.	Children	£1
	Glamour	£2
Barker, Cicely M. (CMB)	Children	£2
Barham, S.	Children	£3
Barnes, A.E.	Animals	£3
Barnes, G.L.	Animals	£3
	Comic	£1
Barribal, L.	Children	£3
	Glamour	£3–£5
	Theatre	£10

Barraud, A.	General	30
Bask, W.	General	30
Basch, Arpad	Art Nouveau	£80
Bates, Marjorie C.	General	50
Bebb, Rosa	Animals	£2
	General	75
Becker, C.	Military	£6
	Sport	£6
Bee	Comic	30
Beer, Andrew	General	60
Belcher, George	Comic	£4
Bell, Hilda	General	30
Bender, Paul	General	25
Bennett, Godwin	General	25
Beraud, N.	Animals	£1.50
	Military	£3
Berkeley, Edith	General	40
Berthon, Paul	Art Nouveau	£75
Bertiglia, A.	Children	£3
Bianchi	Glamour	£3
Biggar, J.L.	Comic	50

A seasonal greeting from Cecil Aldin £2.50

Billinge, Ophelia	Animals	£1
Billings, M.	General	75
Birch, Nora Annie	Children	50
Bird, H.	Sport	£2.50
Birger	Art Deco	£8
Black, W. Milne (W.M.B.)	Comic	£3
Blair, Andrew	General	40
Bob	Comic	£1
	General	50
Boileau, Philip	Glamour	£3-£4
Bolton, F.N.	General	30
Bompard, S.	Glamour	£4
Borrow, W.H.	General	50
Bothams, W.	General	40
Bottaro, E.	Glamour	£3.50
Bottomley, George	Glamour	£1.50
Boulanger, Maurice	Animals	£4
	Comic	£2
Bourillon	Military	£2
Boutet, Henri	Art Nouveau	£18
Bowden, Doris	Children	£1.50
Bowers, Albert	General	£1
Bowers, S.	General	30
Bowley, M.	Children	£1
Boyne, T.	General	30
Bradshaw, Percy V. (PVB)	Comic	£4
	Political	£5
Braun, W.	Glamour	£5
Breanski, Arthur de	General	60
Brett, Molly	Children	£1
Bridgeman, Arthur W.	General	50
Brisley, Nora	Children	50
Broadrick, Jack	Comic	75
Brown, Maynard	Glamour	£1.50
Browne, Tom	Comic	£2-£3.50
	Poster Ads	£25-£50
	Theatre	£8
	Weekly Telegraph	£5
	Captain Mag	£5
	Cathedrals, etc.	£3.50
Brundage, Frances	Children	
	Chromo-Litho	£6
	Others	£3
	General	£2.50
Brunelleschi, U.	A. Deco	£80
Buchanan, Fred	Comic	£1.50
Buchell, A.	Theatre	£6
Bull, Rene	Comic	£3
Burger, R.	General	40
Burton, F.W.	General	50
Bushby, Thomas	General	40
Busi, Adolfo	Art Deco	£5

Views of Brussels by H. Cassiers £4

Butcher, Arthur	Children	£1.50
	Glamour	£1.50
Buxton, Dudley	Comic	75
Caldecott, Randolph	Children	60
Carey, John	Comic	£1+
Carline, George	General	50
Carnel, Albert	Comic	£1.25
Carrere, F.O.	Glamour	£6
Carruthers, W.	General	50
Carter, Reg	Comic	£1+
Carter, Sydney	Comic	£1.50
Cassiers, H.	General	£4
Cattley, P.R.	Comic	50
Chalker	Comic	50
Chandler, E.	Comic	£1
Charlet, J.A.	Glamour	£5
Chatterton, F.J.S.	Animals	£1.50
Cherubini, M.	Glamour	£1.50
Chidley, Arthur	Military	£2.50
Chiostri	Art Deco	£20+
Christiansen, Hans	Art Nouveau	£80
Christie, G.R.	Comic	
	Pre-1918	£1.50
	After 1918	£1

Name	Category	Price
Christy, F. Earl	Glamour	£2.50
Clapsaddle, Ellen H.	Children	£3
	General	£2
Clarkson, R.	General	30
Cloke, Rene	Children	£1.50
Coates, A.	General	30
Cobbe, B.	Animals	£2+
Cock, Stanley	Comic	£2.50
Coffin, Ernest	Exhibitions	£2
Colborne, Lawrence	Comic	£1.25
Cole, Edwin	General	30
Coleman, W.S.	Children	£2.50
Colombo, E.	Glamour	£3
	Children	£2
Combaz, Gisbert	Art Nouveau	£70
Comicus	Comic	75
Cooper, A. Heaton	General	50
Cooper, Phyllis	Children	£3
Copping, Harold	Glamour	£2
Corbella, T.	Glamour	£5
Cordingley, G.R.	General	40
Corke, C. Essenhigh	General	50
Cottom, C.M.	Children	£2
Cowham, Hilda	Children	£1.50
	Comic	£1.50
Crackerjack	Comic	£1.50
Cramer, Rie	Art Deco	£12
Cremieux, Suzanne	Glamour	£5
	Military	£5
Croft, Anne	General	25
Crombie, C.M.	Comic	£2.50
Croxford, W.E.	General	30
Cubley, H. Hadfield	General	50
Cumming, Neville	Shipping	£1.50–£2.50
Cynicus	Comic Court Sized	£10
	Early U/B	£2
	Last train, etc.	£1.50
	Later	£1.25
Daniell, Eva	Art Nouveau	£55
Dauber	Comic	£1.50
Davey, George	Comic	£1.50
Daws, F.T.	Animals	£1
Dexter, Marjorie M.	Children	50
Diefenbach, K.W.	Glamour	£8
Diemer, Michael Zeno	General	£6
Dinah	Children	40
Dink	Sport	£3.50
Dirks, Gus	Comic	75
Dobson, H.J.	General	40
Döcker, E, Jnr	Art Nouveau	£40
Donadini jr.	Animals	£2
Douglas, J.	General	30
Driscoll	Comic	30
Drummond, Eileen	Animals	£1.50
Drummond, Norah	Animals	£2
Ducane, E. & F.	General	40
Duddle, Josephine	Children	£2
Dudley, Tom	General	40

TORBOLE VOM MONTE BALDO.

M. Zeno Diemer £6

Name	Category	Price
Dudley	Comic	30
Dufresne, Paul	Glamour	£3
Duncan, Hamish	Comic	75
Duncan, J.	Children	75
Dunn, James S.	Shipping	£2
Dupuis, Emile	Military	£4
Dwiggins, C.V. (Dwig.)	Comic	£4
Dyer, W.H.	General	50
Dymond, R.J.	General	30
Earnshaw, H.C.	Comic	£1.25
Ebner, Pauli	Children	£4
Edgerton, Linda	Children	£1.50
Edwards, Edwin	General	40
Ellam	Comic	£2+
Elliot, Harry	Sport	£5
Emanuel, Frank L.	General	40
Endacott, S.	General	£1.50
Esmond, (Germs)	Comic	£4
F.S.	Comic	75
F.W.	Comic	75
Fabiano, F.	Glamour	£6
Feiertag, K.	Children	£2
Fidler, Alice Luella	Glamour	£2.50
Fidler, Elsie Catherine	Glamour	£2.50
Finnemore, J.	General	60
Fisher, Harrison	Glamour	£3.50
Fitzpatrick	Comic	25
Fleury, H.	Comic	£1
	Railway	£1.50
Flower, Charles E.	General	75
Folkard, Charles	Children	£3
Fontan, Leo	Glamour	£6
Forres, Kit	Children	40
Foster, Gilbert	General	40
Foster, R.A.	General	30
Fradkin, E.	Children	40
French, Annie	Art Deco	£40
Fry, John H.	Ships	£2.50
Fuller, Edmund G.	Comic	£3
Fulleylove, Joan	General	50
Fullwood, A.A.	General	£3
Furniss, Harry	Political	£4
Gallon, R.	General	50
Gardener, E.C. (ECG)	General	50
Gassaway, Katherine	Children	£2
Gay, Cherry	Children	30
Gayac	Glamour	£5
Gear, M.	Animals	75
Gerald, Brian	General	30
Gerbault, H.	Glamour	£4
Gibson, Charles Dana	Glamour	£3
Giglio	Glamour	£3
Gill, Arthur	Comic	£3
Gilmour	Comic	60
Gilson, T.	Comic	£1.25
Gladwin, May	Comic	£1.50
Golay, Mary	General	£1
Goodman, Maud	Children	
	Tuck Chromo-Litho	£6
	Hildersheimer	50
Govey, Lilian	Children	£1
Gozzard, J.W.	General	50
Graeff	Comic	75
Graf, Marte	Art Deco	£5
Grant, Carleton	General	30
Grasset, Eugene	Art Nouveau	£27
Green, Roland	Animals	£1.50
Greenaway, Kate	Children	
	1903 printing	£50
Greiner, M.	Children	£4
Gretty, G.	General	30
Grey, Mollie	Children	30
Grimes	Comic	50
Grosze, Manni	Art Deco	£5
Grunewald	Art Deco	£5
Guerzoni, C.	Glamour	£5
Guillaume	Comic	£3
Gunn, A.	Glamour	£3
Guy, T.	General	30
Hager, Nini	Art Nouveau	£25
Hannaford	General	30
Hansi	Children	£4
Harbour, Jennie	Art Deco	£6
Hardy, Dudley	Comic	£4
	Glamour	£5
Hardy, Florence	Children	£4
Hardy, F.	A. Deco	£5
Hardy, F.C.	Military	£1.50
Hassall, John	Advert	£25-£35
	Comic	£4
	Theatre	£15-£20
Haviland, Frank	Glamour	£3
Hayes, F.W.	General	75
Hayes, Sydney	Animals	£1
Hebblethwaite, S.H.	Comic	£2.50
Henckle, Carl	Military	£4
Henry, Thomas	Children	50
Herouard	Glamour	£8
Hey, Paul	General	£4
Heyermans, John A.	General	30
Hier, Prof. van	General	£1.50
Higham, Sydney	General	75
Hilton, Alf	Comic	75
Hines, B.	General	50

**Canadian view by Charles F. Flower
on Tuck Reward Card £2**

**A New York view by Charles F. Flower.
More for North American Series £2**

Jenkins, G.H.	General	50
Johnson, M.	General	40
Josza, Carl	Art Nouveau	£27
Jotter	General	75
	Hotels	£1.50
	Better Cards	£2
Kainradl, L.	Art Nouveau	£40
Kammerer, R.	General	30
Karaktus	Comic	50
Kaskeline, Fred	Glamour	£2
Kaufmann, J.C.	Animals	£1
Keene, Elmer	General	30
Keene, Minnie	Animals	75
Keesey, Walter M.	General	30
Kempe	Children	£3
Kennedy, A.E.	Animals	£2–£3
	Theatre	£8
	Later issues	£1+
Kidd, Will	Children	£2
King, A. Price	General	50
King, Jessie M.	Art Nouveau	£40
Kinnear, J.	General	40
Kinsella, E.P.	Children	£1.50–£5
	Comic	£1.50–£5
	Theatre	£8

Hodgson, W. Scott	General	20
Hoffmann, H.	General	40
Hohenstein, A.	Art Nouveau	£15
Holloway, Edgar A.	Military	£2
Horrell, Charles	Glamour	£1.50
Horsfall, Mary	Glamour	£2
Horwitz, Helena	Glamour	£2.50
Howard, C.T.	General	75
Hudson, Gerald	Military	£2
Hughes, Lloyd	Comic	50
Hunt, Edgar	Animals	£1
Hunt, Muriel	Animals	£1.50
Hunter, Mildred C.	Animals	£1
Hurst, Hal	Comic	£1.50
Hutchinson, F.	General	40
Hyde, Graham	Comic	£2.50
Ibbetson, Ernest	Comic	£3
	Military	£3
Innes, John	Ethnic	£2
Jackson, Helen	Children	£3
Jacobs, Helen	Children	£4
James, Frank	Animals	50
James, Ivy Millicent (IMJ)	Children	£3
Jarach, A.	Glamour	£6
Jay, Cecil	Glamour	£2.50

Graham Hyde 'Oilette' Series 6458 £2.50

A typical S. Endacott (Worth's Series) £1.50

13

Kirchner, Raphael	Art Nouveau	
	Early £50	
	Glamour	
	Middle Period . . £25	
	Bruton Galleries . £12	
Kirk, A.H.	General 40	
Kirkpatrick	General 50	
Kirmse, Persis	Animals £1.50	
Klein, Christina	General	
	Chromo-Litho . £2.50	
	Later issues . . . £1	
Kley, Paul	General £5	
Koch, Ludwig	Sport £3.50	
Koehler, Mela	Art Deco £18	
Konopa	Art Nouveau £18	
Kosa	Art Nouveau £65	
Kulas, J.V.	Art Nouveau £30	
Kyd	Comic . . . . . . £3+	
	Literary £6	
Lacy, Chas. J. de	Shipping £2.50	
Lamb, Eric	General 40	
Lambert, H.G.C.Marsh-	Children . £1.50–£2.50	
Larcombe, Ethel	Art Nouveau . . . £20	
Lasalle, Jean	Glamour £2	
	General 50	
Lauder, C.J.	General 40	
Lautrec, H. de Toulouse	Art Nouveau . £300–£500	
Lawes, H.	General 40	
Leete, Alfred	Comic £1.50	
Lehmann, Felix	Sport £3	
Leigh, Conrad	Military 50	
LeMunyon, Pearle Fidler	Glamour £2.50	
Leonnec, G.	Glamour £6	
Lessieux, E. Louis	Art Nouveau . . . £27	
Lester, Adrienne	Animals 75	
Lester, Ralph	Glamour £2	
Lewin, F.G.	Comic . . . . . £1+	
Lilien	General £4	
Lindsell, L.	General £1	
Lloyd, T. Ivester	Glamour £3	
Long, L.M.	General 20	
Longley, C.	Art Deco £15	
Longstaffe, Ernest	General 50	
Loreley	Art Deco £10	
Lowe, Meta	Children 75	
Ludgate	Comic 50	
Ludovici, Albert	Children . . . £3	
Ludovici, Alan J.	Comic £2.50	
	Political £3	

Marte Graf not to be confused with Manni Grosze £5

M.S.M.	Glamour £15	
Mac	Animals £1	
	Comic 50	
Macdonald, A.K.	A. Nouveau . . . £15+	
Mackain, F.	Comic 75	
Macleod, F.	Comic 75	
McGill, Donald	Comic	
	Early dated . . £2.50	
	Pre-1914 . . . £1.50	
	Later 75	
	'New' 10	
McIntyre, R.F.	General 40	
McNeill, J.	Military £2	
Maggs, J.C.	Coaching 75	
Maguire, Bertha	General 50	
Maguire, Helena	Animals . . . . . £3+	
	General 60	
Mailick, A.	General £3	

Name	Category	Price
Mair, H. Willebeek le	Children	£5
Mallet, Beatrice	Children	75
Manavian, V.	Comic	£1
Marco, M.	Glamour	£1.50
Marechaux, C.	Glamour	£3
Margetson, Hester	Children	£1.50
Martin, L.B.	Comic	40
Martineau, Alice	General	£1.50
Martino, R. de	General	50
Mason, Finch	Comic	£1.50
	Sport	£2
Mastroianni, D.	General	50
Mataloni, G.	Art Nouveau	£15
Matthison, W.	General	30
Maurice, Reg	Comic	75
Mauzan, A.	Children	£2
	Glamour	£4
May, Phil	Comic	
	Write-aways	£4
	Oilette	£2.50
Maybank, Thomas	Children	£2
Mead-Gibbs	Shipping	£1.25
Mercer, Joyce	Art Deco	£5
Meredith, Jack	Comic	50
Merte, O.	Animals	£2
Meschini, G.	Art Deco	£10
Metlicovitz, L.	Art Nouveau	£15
Meunier, Henri	Art Nouveau	£70
Meunier, Suzanne	Glamour	£8+
Miller, Hilda T.	Children	£2.50–£5+
Milliere, Maurice	Glamour	£6
Mills, Ernest H.	Animals	£1.50
Monestier, C.	Glamour	£3
Montague, R.	General	40
Montedoro, M.	A. Deco	£15
Moore, F.	Railway	75
Moreland, Arthur	Comic	£2
	Political	£4
Morgan, F.E.	Comic	75
Morris, M.	General	75
Moser, Koloman	Art Nouveau	£60
Mostyn, Dorothy	Glamour	£2
Mostyn, Marjorie	Glamour	£2
Mouton, G.	Glamour	£5
Mucha, Alphonse	Art Nouveau	£75+
Nailod, C.S.	Glamour	£4
Nam, Jacques	Glamour	£6
Nanni, G.	Glamour	£5
Nap	Comic	£1
Nash, A.A.	Children	£1.50
Nerman	Art Deco	£6
	Theatre	£12
Newton, G.E.	General	40
Ney	Glamour	£6
Nielsen, Vivienne	Animals	£1.50
Nixon, K.	Children	£2.50
Noble, Ernest	Comic	£1
Norman, Parsons	General	75
Norwood, A. Harding	General	30
Noury, Gaston	A. Nouveau	£30
Nystrom, Jenny	Glamour	£4
O'Beirne, F.	Military	£8+
O'Neill, Rose	Children	£4
Opper, F.	Comic	75
Orens, Denizard	Political	£20
Outcault, R.F.	Children	£1.25
	Comic	£1.50
Outhwaite, Ida R.	Children	£3
Owen, Will	Comic	£3.50
	Theatrical	£6
Palmer, Phyllis M.	Children	£1.50
Palmer, Sutton	General	40
Pannett, R.	Glamour	£1.50
	Theatre	£6+

One Moment, Sir!

Will Owen with camera theme £3.50

Artist	Category	Price
Parker, N.	Animals	75
Parkinson, Ethel	Children	£4+
Parlett, Harry	Comic	75
Parlett, T.	Comic	50
Parr, B.F.C.	General	20
Parsons, F.J.	Railway	£1
Paterson, Vera	Children	75
Patella, B.	Art Nouveau	£15
Payne, Arthur C.	General	50
Payne, G.M.	Glamour	£1.50
	Advertising	£6–£8
	Comic	£1.25+
Payne, Harry	Horses	
	Tuck's Early	£15–£20
	Oilette	£2.50
	Military	
	Tuck's Early	£8–£25
	Oilette	£2–£15
	Badges & Wearers	£6–£15
	Stewart & Woolfe	£8
	Gale & Polden	£6–£8
	Rural	£2–£10
	Coaching	£8–£12
	Metropolitan Police	£15–£20
	Wild West	£8

See 1981 Edition for full listing and 1982 for Amendments.

Artist	Category	Price
Pearse, Susan B.	Children	£3.50+
Peddie, Tom	Glamour	75
Pellegrini, E.	General	£2
Peltier, L.	Glamour	£5
Penley, Edwin A.	General	40
Penny, Theo	Comic	75
Penot, A.	Glamour	£6
Pepin, Maurice	Glamour	£5
Peras	Glamour	£5
Percival, E.D.	General	40
Perlberg, F.	Animals	£1.50
Perly	Comic	30
Person, Alice Fidler	Glamour	£2.50
Pfaff, C.	General	£3
Phillimore, R.P.	General	£4
Phipson, E.A.	General	50
Pinder, Douglas	General	20
Pinkawa, Anton	Art Nouveau	£25
Piper, George	Children	60
Pirkis	Comic	
	Coloured	£2.50
	B/W	£1.50

Artist	Category	Price
Plumstead, Joyce	Children	£1.50
Pope, Dorothy T.	Animals	£4
Popini	Art Nouveau	£20
Poulbot, Francisque	Children	£2
Preston, Chloe	Children	£1.50+
Purser, Phyllis	Children	£1
Pyp	Comic	£2
Quatremain, W.W.	General	50
Quinnell, Cecil W.	Glamour	£2
Quinton, A.R.	General	75
	Tuck Oilettes	£1.25
Quinton, F.E.	General	30
Quinton, Harry	Comic	75
Raemaekers, Louis	Political	£2
Rambler	General	30
Ramsey, George S.	General	30
Rankin, George	Animals	£1.50
Rappini	Glamour	£3
Rauh, Ludwig	Glamour	£10
Reckling, L.C.	General	40
Reichert, C.	Animals	£1.50
Reiss, Fritz	General	£4
Reynolds, Frank	Comic	£3
Ribas	Glamour	£6
Richardson, Agnes	Children	£2+
Richardson, R.E.	General	50
Right	Comic	75
Ritter, Paul	General	£2.50
Roberts, Violet M.	Comic/Animals	£5
Robida, A.	General	£3
Robinson, W. Heath	Comic	£3
Rodella, G.	Glamour	£3
Rose, Freda Mabel	Children	50
Rosenvinge, Odin	Shipping	£3
Rossi, J.C.	Art Nouveau	£30
Rostro	Political	£6
Rousse, Frank	General	40
Rowland, Ralph	Comic	£1
Rowlandson, G.	General	£1
Rowntree, Harry	Comic	£3
Rylander	Art Deco	£8
Sager, Xavier (Salt Lake)	Glamour	£6
Salmony, G.	Glamour	£3
Sand, Adina	Glamour	£3
Sandford, H. Dix	Children	£1.50
	Coons	£2.50
Sauber	General	£4

Artist Section continued on page 26

FINE FEATHERS
MAKE FINE BIRDS!

1

CANADIAN PACIFIC

TO THE CANADIAN FARM
INSIST ON TRAVELLING BY C·P·R
Agents
PARK & CO., 80, QUEEN STREET, EXETER

2

BOVRIL

"Alas! my poor Brother"

3

Uganda
Railway

4

EUROPE

AIR FRANCE

5

TRANSVAAL
AUSTELLUNG.

Berlin 1897.

6

7

i

8

LORD BYRON

9

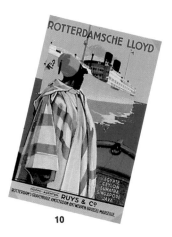

10

11

12

13

14

15

Here are more of the stars, as the shield, In the battle for honor he never will yield.

16

THE AMERICAN GIRL IN JAPAN

17

The Stripes for-ever, long may they wave, O'er the land of the free and the home of the brave.

He stands firm on his feet since his birth; They are large enough to cover the earth.

18

19

20

21

22

23

24

25

26

27

28

29

30

31

32

33

34

35

36

37

38

39

40

41

42

43

44

45

46

47

48

49

50

51

52

53

54

KEY TO COLOUR SECTION

1 A Violet Roberts Cat in the Celesque Series. Pub. Photochrom Co. Ltd £5
2 Canadian Pacific Railway Poster £6
3 H.M. & Co.'s 'Famous Posters in Miniature', Series 4421 . . . . £30
4 Poster for Uganda Railway Lake Steamer & Motor Service £12
5 Air France reproduction of a poster, about 1950. . . . . £8
6 Official Postcard for a German Exhibition, 1897. . . . . £15
7 Chromolithograph by Georg Mühlberg. Pub. Marke. £15
8 American Red Cross Appeal Poster, 1953. . . . . £2.50
9 Coloured Fantasy Head. One of a series of Famous Poets. £30
10 Shipping Co. Poster for Rotterdam–Lloyd. £15
11 Lawson Wood's 'Prehistoric Pastimes' Pub. Davidson, Serie 6106. . . . . £3
12 Unsigned Tuck 'Oilette' Series 9566, 'Diabolo.' £2.50
13 'Bridge' Illustrated – one of a series by Stanley Cock. Pub. Gale & Polden Ltd. (Playing Cards). £5
14 G. E. Studdy's 'Bonzo.' Pub. Valentine, about 1925. £3
15 Chromolithograph signed 'Rother'. Pub. by Stengal & Co. Ser. 10. . . . . £12
16 Valentine's 'Days of the Week' Series. Illustrated is 'Thursday.' £3.50
17 American Girl by Harrison Fisher. Pub. Reinthal & Newman, N.Y. £3.50
18 Art Deco by Joyce Mercer. Pub. C. W. Faulkner & Co. Ltd., 1930s. £6
19 'Uncle Sam' Composite. Pub. in 1906 by Franz Huld, N.Y. £45
20 Embossed 'St Patrick's Day' Greeting. Philco Series No. 3650. . . . . £3
21 Masonic Interest. Copyrighted by Ullman Mfg. Co., N.Y. in 1908. . . . . £3.50
22 Valentine from Tuck's 'Heart & Mind' Series No. 6815. . . . . £4
23 Costumes & Greetings from Hessen. Undivided back chromolithograph. £5
24 WW1 Embroidered Silk In Memory of H.M.S. *Hampshire*. £25
25 Watercolour by S. R. Badmin. Pub. by Royle Publications Ltd. for the Festival of Britain, 1951. . . . . £1.50
26 Court-size card for Windsor Hotel, Glasgow, c1898. . . . . £10
27 Greetings card by Swedish artist Jenny Nyström. £3
28 Boy Scout theme by Laurence Colbourne. Pub. E. Mack, c1916. . . . . £4
29 Fine Chromolithograph. Pub. Meissner & Buch, Leipzig, Serie 1149. . . . . £6
30 One of the 'Tosca' Series by L. Metlicovitz. Pub. G. Ricordi & C., Milan. £10
31 Printed on velvet paper in Japan, for Formosa Oolong Tea Rooms. £15
32 Official Card for the Lake Garda Steamer Company. £15
33 No 36 of the 'Collection des Cent' (One of the major postcard series) Artist A. Cadiou. £80
34 One of a long series of Jugoslav costumes. Pub. in Zagreb. £1
35 Charming Art Deco card by Mela Koehler. Published in Austria. £18
36 The artist has not been positively identified (L. Merfil?) Pub. Leo Stainer, Innsbruck. £3
37 Tuck 'Art' Postcard Series 1036 by L. Balestrieri., undivided back. £5
38 Italian Art Deco by artist L. Mauzan. £5
39 Tuck 'Oilette' Series 9098 'The Homes of Literary Men.' Watercolours by Sydney Carter. £1.50
40 Edward VII & Queen Alexandra's Coronation Robes. Pub. by Gale & Polden Ltd. £1.50
41 A patriotic Swedish card Pub. by Axel Eliasson, Stockholm. £5
42 A French Boer War cartoon. Publisher unknown. £15
43 Japanese card commemorating Prince Arthur's visit to Japan. £8
44 Christmas card for 1900 commemorating 63 years of Queen Victoria's reign. £25
45 Card for the 1956 Olympic Games in Australia. £3.50
46 The unmistakeable line of artist Harry Eliott on this early French-published card. £5
47 Tuck's 'Empire Postcard' No. 262, with embossed flags. Published during the Boer War.
   This one used on 6 June 1900. . . . . £14
48 Poster-type for Union-Castle Line. £20
49 Cartoon by Fred Buchanan, published after 1902. . . . . £4
50 WW1 Patriotic. Pub. by E. Mack. (No 1427) London. £1.50
51 American Patriotic. Pub. by Illustrated Postal Card & Nov. Co., N.Y. £1.50
52 London Underground Poster showing views of Dickens' London. £40
53 Andrew Reid & Co. card for L. & S.W. Rly. Co. Ships. £18
54 Poster-type card for Hong Kong & Shanghai Hotels Ltd. £5

Schonflug, Fritz	Comic	£3
Schubert, H.	Glamour	£3
	General	£3
Schweiger, L.	General	£4
Scottie	Glamour	£4
Scrivener, Maude	Animals	£1.50+
Severn, Walter	General	50
Shand, C.E.	Art Deco	£6
Shaw, W. Stocker	Comic	£1
Shelton, S.	General	30
Shepheard, G.E.	Comic	£1.50+
Shoesmith, Kenneth	Shipping	£2.50–£3.50
Simkin, R.	Military	£8
Simonetti, A.M.	Glamour	£3
Small, D.	General	£1
Smith, Jessie Wilcox	Art Deco	£12
	Children	£5
Smith, Syd	Comic	50
Smyth, D. Carlton	Children	£1.50
Somerville, Howard	Glamour	£3
Sonrel, Elisabeth	Art Nouveau	£28
Sowerby, Millicent	Children	£3.50
	Chromo-litho	£5
Spatz	Comic	£1
Sperlich, T.	Animals	£2
Spurgin, Fred	Comic/Patriotic	£2+
	Glamour	£3
Stannard, H.	General	40
Stead, A.	General	20
Steele L.	Children	75
Steinlen, Alexandre	Art Nouveau	£60
Stenberg, Aina	Art Nouveau	£8
Sternberg, V.W. (VWS)	Children	£1.25
Stewart, J.A.	Military	£2.50
Stoddart, R.W.	Comic	75
Stokes, G. Vernon	Animals	75
Stower, Willi	Shipping	
	Early	£8–£10
	Later	£3
Stretton, Philip	Animals	£2
Studdy, G.E.	Comic	£1.50
	Bonzo	£3
Syd	Comic	75
Symonds, Constance	Children	£2
T.B.M.	Comic	50
Tait	Comic	40
Talboys, A.	Animals	£1.50
Tam, Jean	Glamour	£6
Tarrant, Margaret W.	Children	£1+
Taylor, A.	Comic	30
	Children	35

Tempest, D.	Children	75
	Comic	75
Tempest, Margaret	Children	75
Terzi, A.	Glamour	£5
Thackeray, Lance	Comic	
	Write-away	£4
	Oilettes	£2.50
Thiede, Adolf	General	£1
Thiele, Arthur	Animals	£6
	Comic	£6
Thomas, Bert	Comic	£1.50
Thompson, E.H.	General	40
Thorne, Diana	Animals	75
Toussaint, M.	Military	£6
Trick, E.W.	General	20
Trow	Comic	20
Turrian, E.D.	Art Nouveau	£22
Twelvetrees, C.H.	Children	£1.75
Uden, E.	General	40
Underwood, Clarence F.	Glamour	£2
Upton, Florence K.	Children	£8+
	Later issues	£10+
	Tuck Oilettes	£10+

T. Sperlich £2

Name	Category	Price		Name	Category	Price
Usabal, Luis	Glamour	£3		Wishaw, M.C. (MCW)	General	£2+
Vallet, L.	Glamour	£5		White, Brian	Children	50
Valter, Eugenie M.	Animals	£1		White, Flora	Children	£1.50
Valter, Florence E.	Animals	£1		Wichera, R.R.	Children	£3
Vaughan, E.H.	General	40			Glamour	£4
Voellmy, F.	General	£3		Wiederseim, G.G.	Children	£4
Wain, Louis	Animals			Wielandt, Manuel	General	£4
	Vignettes used	£8		Wilcock, A.M.	Children	£1.50
	Vignettes unused	£12+		Wilkin, Bob	Comic	40
	Later issues	£10+		Williams, Madge	Children	75
	Tuck Oilettes	£10+		Williams, Warren	General	40
Walker, F.S.	General	40		Wimbush, Henry B.	General	50
Walker, Hilda	Animals	£1.50		Wimbush, Winifred	General	50
Wanke, Alice	Art Deco	£10		Wood, Lawson	Comic	£2
	Children	£5			Prehistoric	£3
Ward, Dudley	Comic	£1			Gran'pop	£2.50
Ward, L. (Spy)	Political	£3		Wood, Starr	Comic	£3+
Ward, Herbert	Military	£2.50		Woodville, R. Caton	Military	£2.50
Ward, Vernon	General	40		Wright, Gilbert	General	75
Wardle, Arthur	Animals	£1.50		Wright, Seppings	General	40
Warrington, E.	General	30		Wuyts, A.	Children	£3
Watson, C.M. West	Animals	£1.25			Glamour	£4
Wealthy, R.J.	Animals	£1.50		Young, A.	General	50
West, A.L.	Animals	£1		Hayward Young, (Jotter)	General	£1.50
West, Reginald	General	30		Hayward Young, Gwen	General	£1.50
Wheeler, Dorothy	Children	£1+		Zandrino, Adelina	Glamour	£5
				Zirka, C.	Glamour	£3

One of many hundreds of similar views by Manuel Wielandt £4

Electric lighting promotion. This poster £25

'Shell' posters – this one unnumbered £35

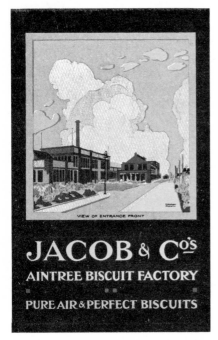

Art Deco advertising was a feature of the thirties.
This, £15

Fuller's Ad, with exhibition interest £25

ADVERTISING

POSTER DESIGNS

This section includes cards actually used for advertising promotion as well as those like Tuck's Celebrated Posters which were well-known posters produced in miniature and published in sets or series for collectors. Many thousands of different designs exist, too numerous to list. Prices vary and you would expect to pay more for popular series, well-known or collectable products and cards designed by prominent artists such as John Hassall, Kinsella, Cecil Aldin, Tom Browne, etc. All cards listed are coloured, except where otherwise indicated.

Tuck's Celebrated Posters
Common designs. e.g.
    Dewar's, Cadbury's, etc £15
Other designs
    (later series are rarer) . . . £30–£75
Bryant & May's £15
Campbell's Soups (Weidersheim) . . £30
Camp Coffee £35
Continental Tyres £30
C.W.S. £10
Fry & Sons . . . . £20–£40
    T. Browne designs £15
Gossage's Soap £35
Holbrooks Ltd. £18
Horniman's Tea . . . . . . £20–£25
H.M. & Co's Famous Posters . . . £30
Keiller, James £12
Nestlés Milk . . . . £25–£35
North British Rubber Co. £30
Raleigh Cycles £20
St Ivel Cheese £12
Shell £35
Shell (reprints set) £1
Skipper Sardines . . . . £8+
Tit-bits £2
Viscan Pet Foods £5
Wood Milne Rubber Heels . . . £15+

TOBACCO
Adkins Tobacco
    (Tom Browne posters) £50

Grays Cigarettes (views) £1
R. & J. Lea (Chairman's series) . . £2.50
    with suppliers' imprint £4
Ogdens £40
Philips, Godfrey 35
Sarony, Nicholas 75
Wills £40

Aviation
Circus
Motoring . . . *see under these headings*
Railway
Shipping
Theatre

GIVE AWAYS, etc.
These are cards distributed by the advertisers either as 'give aways' or in exchange for tokens. Subjects are varied and rarely have any connection with the product advertised. Some firms merely overprinted their blurb or names onto existing cards with or without the publishers' consent!

Amami Shampoo 75
Airlines . . . . £1.50+
Beecham's Pills (views) 75
Bees Ltd 30
Boon's Cocoa (views) 75
Bovril (art repros) 75
Broma Cocoa (plantation sketches) . 75
Butywave Shampoo (film stars) . . . £1
Cadbury's – Butterflies £2
Caillers, F. (views) 30
Canadian – Dept. of Emigration . . £1.50
Capern's Bird Food (birds) 75
Carter's Seeds 30
Chamberlin & Smith 30
Chelsea Flower Show 50
Chivers & Sons (fruit) 75
Chocolat Lombat £1.50
Clay Cros Co. Mining –
    Topographical £6
Colman's Starch £2.50
Cook, E. (aviation interest) £6
Cope's 25
Daily Mirror (beauty contest) 50
Daily Express 50

No. 108.] **A ROADMAKER.** [See No. 125.
A Clay Cross Collier cutting a road for the transit from
the workings to the shaft of the renowned "C.X.C. Gold
Medal" Coal.

Clay Cross Co giveaway. One of a series of mining
scenes £6

**REGULAR DELIVERIES OF ANY
QUANTITY FROM 1 CWT. UPWARDS**

A 'Giveaway' poster card for the topographical
collector – Baldwins of Bristol £10

Daily Sketch	75	Lemco Coronation Postcards	£15
De Beukelaer's Cocoa	50	Lemco Cattle (Hassall)	£6
Elliman's Linament (Tuck)	£2.50	Lever Bros. (Port Sunlight)	75
Field, J.	£1.50	Lipton Tea	75
Fine Arts Pub. Co.	30	Maggi (views)	30
Fry, J. S. (non-poster)	£4	Menier	25
G.P. Govt. Tea (composite)	£120	Mellin's Food	£4
Garden City Ass.	£2.50	Molassine Meal	£2.50
Glaxo	£1	Nestlés	£2
Goss, W. H.	£4	New Departure Coaster Hub	
Guinness, A.	£3	(G. M. Payne)	£8
Guinness, A. (production scenes) . .	£2	New Zealand Tourist Dept.	75
Hadfield, George & Co.	50	New Zealand Lamb	30
Hartley, W.P.	75	N. British Rubber Co. (golf)	£7
Haydock Coals	30	Ocean Accident Corp.	£2
Heinz, J. & Co.	£12	Odd Fellows Friendly Society	£4
Horniman's Tea (views)	£1	Odol Dentifrice (actresses)	£1.50
Horniman's Tea (invisible picture) . .	£4	Oetzmann's Cottages	£1.50
Imperial Fine Art Co.	30	Old Calabar	£1.50
International Horse Show	£4	Oxo	£4
Jacob, W.	75	Peark's	75
King Insurance Co. (Kings & Queens)	£4	Pears, A. & F. (Bubbles)	30

Peek Frean (invisible picture) £4
Pertab Sinjh & Zenia Co. 60
Phoenix (poultry foods) £6
Pickfords (transport) N.B. Have been reprinted £6
Pitman Health Food Co. £1
Price's Candles (battle scenes) . . . £4
Price's Candles (nursery riddles) . . £6
Quaker Oat Smiles £8
Reckitts (naval) £4
Ridgway's Tea £1
Radio Ham (call sign cards) £1
Rowntree £1
St. Bartholomew's Hospital 20
St. Ivel (views) 50
St. Paul's Hospital 20
Selfridge Co. £1.50
Shippam's 75
Singer Sewing Machines
    Aircraft £3
    Battleships £1.50
    Other types 50
Spratt's Dog Food £1
Suchard Chocolate – early vignettes . £20
Sutton & Sons 75
Symington & Co. (foreign views) . . 60
Thorley (photo type) £1.50
Trent Pottery £2.50
Ty-Phoo Tea (Oilette type
    views and animals) . . . . £1+
    Items seen all carry bulk posting postmarks.
Van Houten's Cocoa 50
Zoo Adverts £1
Zoological Society Adverts £1.50

INSERTS
Cards produced by or given away with newspapers and magazines to woo readers and increase circulation.

Brett Publications 30
Canary & Cage Bird Life 50
Captain Magazine (Tom Browne) . . £5
Christian Novels 20
Connoisseur Magazine 30
Daily News Wallet Guide 30
Dainty Novels 50
Princess Novels 20
Shurey's Pub. 30
Sketchy Bits 20
Smart Novels 20
T.A.T. 75
Tiny Tots 75

THE QUEEN.

Milkmaid Milk Reward Card chromo-lithograph with biographical details on back £3.50

Ward Lock 75
Weekly Tale-Teller 20
Weekly Telegraph
    (Tom Browne sketches) £5
Weldon's Bazaar £2.50
    Coronation Souvenir 1902 . . . . £8
Yes or No 20

REWARD POSTCARDS
Cadbury Bros (birds) £3
Cadbury Bros (butterflies) £3
Cadbury Bros (map cards) £6
Milkmaid Milk £3.50
Nectar Tea £4
Reckitt & Sons Brano
    Reward cards (Heroes & Heroines) £4
Scott's Emulsion £3.50
Hampshire County Council 75
London County Council 50
Oxfordshire Education Committee . . £1
School Board for London £1
Surrey Education Committee 75

Maude Scrivener £1.50

A 'Spratts' F.T. Daws thus £1.50

Norah Drummond £2

Eileen Drummond £1.50

'Mac' £1.50 for cats

F.J.S. Chatterton

Arthur Thiele £6

Hilda Walker £1.50

ANIMALS

GENERAL

The prices in this section are generally for the more common types, usually photographic, greetings types and poorer quality printed. It should be noted, as forecast last year, that there has been a tremendous rise in the popularity of these cards.

Animals – wild	30–50
Animals – dressed	75–£1
Birds	50–75
Butterflies	£1–£1.50
Cats	30–60
Cattle (cows, etc.)	25–50
Dogs	50–£1
Donkeys	35+
Fish	50
Horses	50
Working	75–£1.50
Zoo Animals	75+
Officials	£1+

Farmyard animals by an under-rated artist £1

Tuck's British Butterflies Series 9497.
Very popular this year £1.50

ARTISTS

Ackroyd, W.M.	£1.50
Ainsley, Anne	50
Aldin, Cecil	£3
Ambler, C.	50
Anders, O.	£2+
Austin, E.H.S. Barnes	£4
Austin, Winifred (birds)	75
Barnes, A. E.	£3
Barnes, G. L.	£3
Bebb, Rosa	£2
Beraud, N.	£1.50
Billinge, Ophelia	£1
Boulanger, Maurice	£4
Chatterton, F.J.S.	£1.50
Cobbe, B.	£2+
Daws, F.T.	£1
Donaldini, Jr.	£2
Gear, M.	75
Drummond, Norah	£2
Drummond, Eileen	£1.50
Green, Roland	£1.50
Hayes, Sidney	£1

This is 'Bunny's Little Love Affair' Tuck Series 3362. £1.50 You'll find this artist listed in 'Comics' at 75p!

Louis Wain's cats with human dress and behaviour. This Tuck £12

Hunt, Edgar	£1
Hunt, Muriel	£1.50
Hunter, Mildred C.	£1
James, Frank	50
Kaufmann, J. C.	£1
Keene, Minnie	75
Kennedy, A. E.	£2–£3
Kirmse, Persis	£1.50
Lester, Adrienne	75
Mac	£1
Maguire, Helena	£3+
Merte, O.	£2
Mills, Ernest, H.	£1.50
Nielsen, Vivienne	£1.50
Parker, N.	75
Perlberg, F.	£1.50
Pope, Dorothy T.	£4
Rankin, George	£1.50
Reichert, C.	£1.50
Roberts, Violet	£5
Scrivener, Maude	£1.50+
Sperlich, T.	£2

Stokes, G. Vernon	75
Stretton, Philip	£2
Talboys, A.	£1.50
Thiele, A.	£6
Thorne, Diana	75
Valter, Eugenie M.	£1
Valter, Florence E.	£1
Wain, Louis	
Vignette Used*	£8
Unused	£12+
Later issues	£10+
Tuck Oilettes	£10+
Walken, Hilda	£1.50
Wardle, Arthur	£1.50
Watson, C. M. West	£1.25
Wealthy, R. J.	£1.50
West, A. L.	£1

*Used means written on face of card.

Many other artists included animals in their work. These are not usually worth a premium and reference should be made to the 'Comic' and 'Artists' chapters.

ART (DECO, NOUVEAU AND GLAMOUR)

ART DECO
Artists

Birger	£8
Brunelleschi	£80
Busi, Adolfo	£5
Chiostri	£20+
Cramer, Rie	£12
French, Annie	£40
Graf, Marte	£5
Grosze, Manni	£5
Grunewald	£5
Harbour, Jennie	£6
Hardy, F.	£5
Koehler, Mela	£18
Longley, C.	£15
Loreley	£10
Mercer, Joyce	£5
Meschini, G.	£10
Montedoro, M.	£15
Nerman	£6
Rylander	£8
Shand, C.E.	£6

Some remaindered lots have been seen.

Smith, Jessie Wilcox	£12
Stenberg, Aina	£8
Wanke, Alice	£10
Wennenberg, B.	£10

Pierrot by Chiostri. This one above £15

The oriental influence by G. Meschini £10

35

German Art Nouveau by E. Döcker, junior.
In mint condition £40

Viennese Secession Artist Ludwig Kainradl
published by Philipp & Kramer £45

ART NOUVEAU
Artists

Basch, Arpad	£80
Berthon, P.	£75
Boutet, H.	£18
Christiansen, Hans	£80
Combaz, Gisbert	£70
Daniel, Eva	£55
Döcker, E, Jnr	£40
Grasset, Eugene	£27
Hager, Nini	£25
Hohenstein, H.	£15
Jozsa, C.	£27
Kainradl, L.	£40
King, Jessie M.	£40
Kirchner, Raphael (Early)	£50
see also under Glamour	
Konopa	£18
Kosa	£65
Kulas, J.V.	£30
Larcombe, Ethel	£20

Lautrec, Henri de Toulouse	£300–£500
Lessieux, E.L.	£27
MacDonald, A.K.	£15+
Mataloni, G.	£15
Metlicovitz, L.	£15
Meunier, Henri	£70
Moser, Kolomon	£60
Mucha, Alphonse (Mint)	£75+
Noury, Gaston	£30
Patella, B.	£15
Pinkawa, A.	£25
Popini	£20
Rossi, J.C.	£30
Sonrel, Elisabeth	£28
Steinlen, Alexandre	£60
Turrian, E.D.	£22

GLAMOUR
Artists

Abeille, Jack £20
Albertini £4
Asti, Angelo £1.50
Balestrieri, L. £5
Barber, C.W. £2
Barribal, L. . . . . £3–£5
Bianchi £3
Boileau, Philip . . . . £3–£4
Bompard, S. £4
Bottaro, E. £3.50
Bottomley, G. £1.50
Braun, W. £5
Brown, Maynard £1.50
Butcher, A. £1.50
Carrere, F.O. £6
Charlet, J.A. £5
Cherubini, M. £1.50
Christie, F.Earl £2.50
Colombo, E. £3
Copping, H. £2
Corbella, T. £5
Diefenbach, K.W. £8
Dufresne, Paul £3
Fabiano, F. £6
Fidler, Alice Luella £2.50
Fidler, Elsie Catherine £2.50
Fisher, Harrison £3.50
Fontan, Leo £6
Gayac £5
Gerbault, H. £4
Gibson, C.Dana £3
Giglio £3
Guerzonni £5
Gunn, A. £3
Hardy, Dudley £5
Haviland, Frank £3
Herouard £8
Horrell, Charles £1.50
Horsfall, Mary £2
Horwitz, Helena £2.50
Jarach, A. £6
Jay, Cecil £2.50
Kirchner, Raphael
   middle period £25
   Bruton Galleries £12
   see also Art Nouveau
Lasalle, Jean £2
Leonnec, G. £6

Lovely glamour study by Suzanne Meunier £8

Le Munyon, Pearle Fidler £2.50
Lester, Ralph £2
Lloyd, T.Ivester £3
M.S.M. £15
Maillick, A. £3
Marco, M. £1.50
Marechaux, C. £3
Mauzan, A. £4
Meunier, Suzanne £8
Milliere, M. £6
Monestier, C. £3
Mostyn, Dorothy £2
Mostyn, Marjorie £2
Mouton, G. £5
Naillod, C.S. £4
Nam, Jacques £6
Nanni, G. £5
Ney £6
Nystrom, Jenny £4
Pannett, R. £1.50
Payne, G.M. £1.50
Peddie, Tom 75
Peltier, L. £5

L. Usabal £3

Maggy Monier. This artist will be listed next year £6

Penot, A.	£6	Usabal, L.	£3
Pepin, M.	£5	Vallet, L.	£5
Peras	£5	Wichera, R.R.	£4
Person, Alice Fidler	£2.50	Wuyts, A.	£4
Quinnell, Cecil W.	£2	Zandrino, Adelina	£5
Rappini	£3	Zirka, C.	£4
Rauh, Ludwig	£10		
Ribas	£6	**ART REPRODUCTIONS**	
Rodella, G.	£3	(Reproductions of famous paintings)	
Sager, Xavier (Salt Lake)	£6	Black/white	15+
Salmony, G.	£3	Coloured	40+
Sand, Adina	£3	Coloured Chromo-lithographed	£1+
Schubert, H.	£3	Gilt-Edged	Add 50%
Scottie	£4	Museum Cards	10+
Simonetti, A.M.	£3		
Somerville, Howard	£3		
Spurgin, Fred	£3		
Tam, Jean	£6		
Terzi, A.	£5		
Underwood, Clarence E.	£2		

CHILDREN'S CARDS

ARTISTS

Alys, M. £1
Anderson, V. C. £1
Attwell, Mabel Lucie
   Early £2
   Middle £1.50
   Later £1
   Modern Repros 20–40
Azzoni, N. £1
Barber, C. W. £1
Barham, S. £3
Barker, C. M. £2
Barribal, L. £3
Bertiglia, A. £3
Birch, Nora Annie 50
Bowden, Doris £1.50
Bowley, M. £1
Brett, Mollie £1
Brisley, N. 50
Brundage, Frances Chromo-litho . . £6
   Others £3
Butcher, Arthur £1.50

IF YOU CAN'T BE GOOD BE CAREFUL!

Who likes jam? Mabel Lucie Attwell £1.50

Caldecott, Randolph 60
Clapsaddle, E. H. £3
Cloke, Rene £1.50
Coleman, W. S. £2.50
Colombo, E. £2
Cooper, Phyllis £3
Cottom, C. M. £2
Cowham, Hilda £1.50
Dexter, Marjorie 50
Dinah 40
Duddle, Josephine £2
Duncan, J. Ellen 75
Ebner, Pauli £4
Edgerton, Linda £1.50
Feiertag, K. £2
Folkard, Charles £3
Forres, Kit 40
Fradkin, E. 40
Gassaway, Katherine £2
Gay, Cherry 30
Goodman, Maude
   Chromo-litho £6
   Hildersheimer 50

S. Barham (Faulkner 1814) £3

PUSSY'S IN THE WELL

**Linda Edgerton nursery rhyme published by
Savoury of Bristol £2**

OUR BETTERS

'Bonnets up!' Art-Deco by Chloe Preston, so £2.50

Govey, Lilian	£1
Griener, M.	£4
Greenaway, Kate 1903 printing . . .	£50
Grey, Mollie	30
Hansi	£4
Hardy, Florence	£4
Some sets have been remaindered	
Henry, Thomas	50
James, Ivy Millicent (I.M.J.)	£3
Jackson, Helen	£3
Jacobs, Helen	£4
Kempe	£3
Kidd, Will	£2
Kinsella, E. P.	£1.50–£5
Lambert, H. G. C. Marsh . .	£1.50–£2.50
Lowe, Meta	75
Ludovici, A.	£3
Mair, H. Willebeek Le	£5
Mallet, Beatrice	75
Margetson, Hester	£1.50
Mauzan, A.	£2
Maybank, Thomas	£2

Miller, Hilda T.	
Liberty	£5+
Others	£2.50
Nash, A. A.	£1.50
O'Neill, Rose	£4
Outcault, R. F.	£1.25
Nixon, K.	£2.50
Outhwaite, Ida Renthoul	£3
Palmer, Phyllis M.	£1.50
Parkinson, Ethel	£4+
Paterson, Vera	75
Pearse, Susan B.	£3.50+
Piper, George	60
Plumstead, Joyce	£1.50
Poulbot, F.	£2
Preston, Chloe	£1.50+
Purser, Phyllis	£1
Richardson, Agnes	£2+
Rose, Freda Mabel	50
Sandford, H. Dix	£1.50
(Coons)	£2.50
Smith, D. Carlton	£1.50

Happy Little People but as unsigned Sowerby £2.50

Superb Continental children's card. Used 1901 £4

**Very difficult Tuck Series to find No 3472
Cinderella £5**

**Children playing with toys outside Andersen
air raid shelter June 1941 £2**

Smith, Jessie Wilcox £5
Sowerby, Millicent £3.50
   Chromo-litho £5
Steele, L. 75
Sternberg, V. W. (V.W.S.) £1.25
Symonds, Constance £2
Tarrant, Margaret . . . . £1+
Taylor, A. 35
Tempest, D. 75
Tempest, Margaret 75
Twelvetrees, C. H. £1.75
Upton, Florence (mint condition) . . £8+
Wanke, Alice £5
Wheeler, Dorothy . . . . £1+
White, Brian 50
White, Flora £1.50
Wichera, R. R. £3
Wiederseim, G. G. £4
   Campbell's Soup Advert £30
Wilcock, A. M. £1.50
Williams, Madge 75
Wuyts, A. £3

OTHER TYPES
Elves/Fairies 75
Nursery Rhymes . . . . £1+
Photo Type 25
School Groups (identified) . . . £1.50+

TOYS
Bramber Museum (animals) 75
Dolls (close-up photos) £2
Golliwogs £2
Greetings type 30
Mirror Grange £1
Queen's Dolls' House . . . . £1+
Queen's Dolls' House set £60
Titania's Palace
   Tuck, R. £1.25
   Gale & Polden 75
Toys (close-ups) . . . . £1.50+

NOTABLE UNSIGNED SERIES
'Tuck' Art S. 1156
'Ping-Pong in Fairyland' £5

Match striking humour by Dauber £2

Very much collected Will Owen £3.50

COMICS

ARTISTS

A.E. 75
Adams, Will £1.50
Anders, O £2
Aris, Ernest £2
Austerlitz, E. £2.50
Bairnsfather, Bruce £1.50
Barnes, G.L. £1
Bee 30
Belcher, George £4
Biggar, J.L. 50
Black, W.Milne (W.M.B.) £3
Bob £1
Boulanger, M. £2
Bradshaw, P.V. (P.V.B.) £4
Broadrick, Jack 75
Browne, Tom
    Comic . . . . £2.50–£3.50
    Poster Advt. . . . . £25–£50
    Weekly Telegraph £5
    Captain Mag. £5
    Cathedrals, etc. £3.50
Buchanan, Fred £1.50
Bull, Rene £3
Buxton, Dudley 75
Carey, John . . . . £1+
Carnell, Albert £1.25
Carter, Reg . . . . £1+
Carter, Sidney £1.50
Cattley, P.R. 50
Chalker 50
Chandler, E. £1
Christie, G.R. pre-1918 . . . . . £1.50
    after 1918 . . . . £1
Cock, Stanley £2.50
Colbourne, L. £1.25
Comicus 75
Cowham, H. £1.50
Crackerjack £1.50
Crombie, C.M. £2.50
Cynicus
    Court sized £10
    Early U/B £2
    'Last Train', etc. £1.50
    Later £1.25
Dauber £1.50
Davey, George £1.50
Dirks, Gus 75
Driscoll 30

"Wot abaat it?"
"Wot abaat wot?"
"Wot abaat ittin my Billy abaat?"
"Well wot abaat it?"
"Yus wot abaat it?"

Cockney humour by Dudley Buxton.
This above average £1

Dudley 30
Duncan, Hamish 75
Dwiggins, C.V. (Dwig) £4
Earnshaw, H.C. £1.25
Ellam . . . . £2+
Esmond (Germs Series) £4
F.S. 75
F.W. 75
FitzPatrick 25
Fleury, H. £1
Fuller, Edmund G. £3
Gill, Arthur £3
Gilmour 60
Gilson, T. £1.25
Gladwin, May £1.50
Graeff 75
Grimes 50
Guillaume, A. £3
Hardy, Dudley £4
Hassall, John £4
Hebblethwaite, S.H. £2.50
Hilton, Alf 75

Hughes, Lloyd	50
Hurst, Hal	£1.50
Hyde, Graham	£2.50
Ibbetson, Ernest	£3
Karaktus	50
Kinsella, E.P.	£1.50–£5
Kyd see also Literary	£3+
Leete, Alfred	£1.50
Lewin, F.G.	£1+
Ludgate	50
Ludovici, A.	£2.50
Mac	50
Mackain, F.	75
Macleod, F.	75
McGill, Donald	
Early dated	£2.50
Pre-1914	£1.50
Later	75
'New'	10
Manavian, V.	£1
Martin, L.B.	40
Mason, Finch	£1.50
Maurice, Reg	75
May, Phil 'Write Away'	£4
Oilette	£2.50
Meredith, Jack	50
Moreland, Arthur	£2
Morgan, F.E.	75
Nap	£1
Noble, Ernest	£1
Opper, F.	75
Outcault, R.F.	£1.50
Owen, Will	£3.50
Parlett, Harry	75
Parlett, T.	50
Payne, G.M.	£1.25+
Penny, Theo	75
Perly	30
Pirkis Coloured	£2.50
B/W	£1.50
Pyp	£2
Quinton, Harry	75
Reynolds, Frank	£3
Right	75
Roberts, Violet	£5
Robinson, W. Heath	£3
Rowland, Ralph	£1
Rowntree, Harry	£3
Sandford, H. Dix	£1.50
(Coons)	£2.50

THE "LIMERICK" SERIES.

A young married man of Nunhead,
To a pal very solemnly said,
"Though spliced but a week,
If the truth I must speak,
I heartily wish myself dead!"

Kyd 'Limerick' Series. A popular subject now £4

Schonflug, F.	£3
Shaw, W. Stocker	£1
Shepheard, G.E.	£1.50+
Smith, Syd	50
Spatz	£1
Spurgin, Fred see also Patriotic	£2+
Stoddart, R.W.	75
Studdy, G.E. 'Bonzo'	£3
Others	£1.50
Syd	75
T.B.M.	50
Tait	40
Tylor, A.	30
Tempest, D.	75
Thackeray, Lance –	
Write Away Type	£4
Oilette Type	£2.50
Thiele, A.	£6
Thomas, Bert	£1.50
Trow	20
Wain, Louis see under Animals	
Ward, Dudley	£1

"Where was Moses when the light went out?"
(At a Picture Palace.)

Still popular Fred Spurgin,
this one of Jewish interest £5

Devils – one from Baird's 'Signed' Series £4

Wilkins, Bob	40
Wood, Lawson	
Gran'pop	£2.50
'Prehistoric'	£3
Others	£2
Wood, Starr	£3+

THEMATIC

Aviation	£1+
Cats	50
Children	30
Coons	£1.50+
Cricket	£1–£1.50
Cycling	£1.50+
Dogs	40
Erotic	£1.50
Football	75–£1.50
Golfing	£2–£4
Jewish	£2–£5
Lavatory	40
Limericks	£1.50
Local *see Topographical*	

Military	75–£1.50
Motoring	£1.50+
Negro	£1.50+
Police	£1–£1.50
Scouts	£3–£5
Tennis	75
War Comic 1914–1918	£1
War Comic 1939–1945	£2
Irish	£1
Scottish	50–£1.50
Welsh	50

WRITE AWAY TYPE

Davidson Bros	£2.50
Stewart & Woolfe	£2.50
Tuck, R. & Son	
Early U/B	£4
Later Issues	£2.50

SERIES

Tuck Oilette Pickings from 'Puck'	£4
Good Jokes from 'Punch'	£2.50
Wrench Good Jokes from 'Punch'	£1.50

Greta Garbo in Company £3

Cowboys – avidly collected £2

'And tonight my quest is . . .' with advertising on
back for BBC £2.50

Theatre poster, 'I swear he understands every
word I say!' £10

ENTERTAINMENT

CINEMA

Film Stars

Prices quoted are for **B/W photographs.**
Add **up to double** *for coloured.*

Astaire, Fred	£1.50
Bogart, Humphrey	£3
Chaplin, Charlie	£1.50
(Red Letter Stills)	£1.50
Dietrich, Marlene	£3
Gable, Clark	£1
Garbo, Greta	£3
Harlow, Jean	£2.50
Laurel & Hardy	£4
Lombard, Carole	£1.25
Temple, Shirley	£2.50
Valentino, Rudolf	£1
Wayne, John	£3
West, Mae	£3
Cowboy Stars	£2+
Pre-1930 Stars	75
1930–1950 Stars	£1
1950s to date Stars	50
Film Stills	£1+

See also Autograph Supplement after p 56.

Miscellaneous

Bioscopes (Close up)	£15
Cinemas (Close up)	£10–£15
Felix the Cat	£2.50
Disney Films	£2–£4

CIRCUS

Acts	£2+
Adverts – poster type (Barnum & Bailey)	£25+
Adverts – other type	£10
Buffalo Bill's Wild West poster type	£20
Animals – caged	75
Bands	75
Clowns (Famous)	£5
(Unidentified)	£1.50
Fat Men	£2
Freaks	£2
Midgets	£2
Performers	£1+
Sites (local)	£8

See also Autograph Supplement after p 56.

THEATRICAL

Actors/Actresses	25
Actors Publicity Photos	30
Bernhardt, Sarah	£3+
Coward, Noël	£3
Duncan, Isadora	£10
Irving Memorial	£2+
Langtry, Lily	£5
Adverts, poster type (unsigned) Col.	£8+
Adverts, poster type (unsigned) B/W	£1–£4

Artists		
	Barribal	£10
	Browne, T. (Arcadians)	£8
	Buchel	£6
	Hassall	£15–£20
	Kinsella	£10
	Nerman	£12
	Will Owen	£6
	Pannett, R.	£6+

Playbill reproductions (P/C Back)	£6
Play scenes	£1
Autographs of known stars	£1.50+

See also Autograph Supplement after p 56.

One of the Knight Series. This theatre sadly no longer with us £3

47

Ballet Stars	. . . .	£5+	**VARIETY STARS**	
Ballet Companies	. . . .	£3+	Austin Charles	. . . . £2.50
Ballet, Modern	. . . .	50	Bard, Wilkie	. . . . £2.50
Cabaret	. . . .	£1	Chevelier, A.	. . . . £2.50
Concert Parties, named	. . . .	£1.50+	Chevalier, M.	. . . . £2
Conjurers	. . . .	£5+	Chirgwin	. . . . £2
Escapologists	. . . .	£2–£5	Elliott, G. H.	. . . . £3
Gilbert & Sullivan *see Music*			Leno, Dan	. . . . £2.50
Magicians	. . . .	£8	Little Tich	. . . . £4
Passion Plays (Oberammergau)	. . .	35	Lloyd, Marie	. . . . £4
Signed Actors	. . . .	50	Miller, Max	. . . . £2
Passion Plays (other)	. . . . . .	20	Robey, George	. . . . £1
Pierrots, named	. . . .	£1.50	Stratton, Eugene	. . . . £3
Play Stills, Tuck, R.	. . . .	50	Tilley, Vesta	. . . . £1
Other	. . . .	35	Others	. . . . 75+
Radio Celebrities	. . . . . .	£1.50+		
Speciality Acts	. . . .	£1+		
Stuntmen	. . . .	£1.50		
Theatres (close-up) photo	. . .	£3–£8+		
printed	. . . .	£3–£5		
(interior)	. . . .	£3–£5		
On Piers	. . . .	£2–£5		
Opera Houses	. . . .	£2+		
Ventriloquists	. . . .	£8		

MUFFIN PLAYING CRICKET

Television stars of the fifties £1. Ron Mead used to watch this on TV when he came home from school

ETHNIC & SOCIAL HISTORY

COSTUME

National Dress (Welsh)	75
(Irish)	75
(European)	50
Family Portraits	25
Family Groups	25
Hats	30

ETHNIC GROUPS & CHARACTERS

English & Welsh People *see Rural Life*
Europeans see *Neudin Catalogue*

Indians	50+
Irish	75
(humour)	£1.25
Japanese	30+
(Art types)	75–£2+
Scottish	75
(humour)	50–£1.50
Welsh Ladies	£1–£1.50
S. American Indians	£1–£1.50
N. American Indians	£1.50–£3
Cowboys	£1+
J. Innes	£2
Natives – other countries	75–£1.50

FAIRS/MARKETS

Carnivals	£4–£6+
Exhibitions (Local)	£3+
Cattle Markets	£3–£5
Market Places	£2–£5
Street Markets (Petticoat Lane)	£1.50
Photo (others)	£6–£15
Printed	£2–£5
Seaside Fairs	£1.50+
Street Parades	£3–£5+
Travelling Fairs	£8–£12

FOLKLORE

County Humour	50–£1
Customs	40
County Sayings	50–£1
Dunmow Flitch	£1
Ducking Stools	30
Epitaphs	30
Ghosts	25
Gretna Green	25
Lady Godiva	50–£1
Legends	50

Dieppe fisherman and his house
(see Neudin Catalogue) £8

John Innes – difficult to find in good condition £2

Bournemouth Centenary carnival tram £8.50

Markets – a really superb photographic Thirsk
market. At £12 worth well above catalogue figure

49

LANGUAGE
Esperanto (Oilette Series) £8
(Other types) . . . . £2–£5
See also Greetings

LONDON LIFE
Cries of London (Rotophot) £1.50
Rotary Series . . . . £8–£15
Sauber £6
Tuck, R., Early £8
Tuck, R., Oilette £3
Others . . . . £1–£5

MEDICAL
Hospital wards £3
Nurses . . . . 50–£1.50
Operations . . . . £3+
Red Cross Postcards . . . . . . £2.50+
St. John's Ambulance £1.50

POLICE
Policemen (single) £1.50
Policemen (groups) £1.50
See also Comics

POSTAL
Early Postman c.1900 photo type £1.50+
Later Postman . . . . £1+
Postman with hand cart
(photo type – identified) £15
Postmen of the World £6
Postmen of the British Empire £5
Other Art types . . . . . . £1–£1.50
Postmen – Novelty Pull outs . . . . . £2+
Post Boxes, etc. £1.50
Mail Vans, etc. . . . . £8–£15+
Post Offices *see Topographical*

RELIGION
Organisations
Church Army £1
Salvation Army
(General Booth/Portraits) £1.50
(Other issues) £1.50
Miscellaneous
Clergy/Portraits 20
Evangelists/Vans . . . . £3–£5
Jewish Greetings . . . . £3–£5
Lord's Prayer . . . . £1+

Roman Catholicism
(Popes/Portraits) 50
(Popes/Mourning Cards) £3
Other Religion 20
Missionary Societies
Baptist Missionary Society 40
Church Missionary Society 35
London Missionary Society 30
London Society for Promoting
Christianity among the Jews . . . 60
Religious Tract Society 30
Society for the Propagation
of the Gospel 30
South American Missionary Society . 30
Universities' Mission to Central Africa 30
Other issues (un-named societies) . . 30

**Everybody chases photographic rural life – there are
other types such as this Oilette Series 9351
'Ye Countrymen' £2**

RURAL LIFE

	Photo	Printed
Blacksmith (identified)	£5–£10	£2–£5
Bootmaker	£5–£10	£5
Cliff Climbers	£3–£5	£1–£2
Coracle Fishermen	£2	£1–£2
Children at Play	£1.50+	
Crofters	75–£1.50	75–£1.50
Dalesmen	£1.50	£1.50
Deer Stalking	75–£1.50	75–£1.50
Farmworkers	£2+	£1–£2
Flower farming	75–£1.50	75–£1.50
Flower picking	£4–£6	£3–£5
Fruit picking	£4–£6	£3–£5
Gipsies		
Camps	£3–£10	£2–£5
On the road	£8–£15+	£3–£10
Hop pickers	£5–£8	£3–£5
Harvesting	75	75+
Herdsman	50+	50
Hermits	£3–£6	£1.50–£3
Lambing	50+	50
Lace making	£3–£5	£2+
Lavender Fields	75	75
Peat digging	£1–£2+	£1–£2
May Day Celebrations, identified	£3–£5	£3+
Ox Carts	£3	£2
Roasts	£5+	£5
Ploughing	£1.50–£2.50	75
Reaping	£1.50	75
Sheep shearing	£3–£5	£1.50
Sheep dip	£3–£5	£1.50
Spinning & Weaving	£2–£3	£1+
Stocks	60	40
Village Crafts	£2–£5+	£1–£3
Village Folk	£2–£5	£1–£2
Village Life – Oilette type		£2
Water Carriers	£4–£8	£2–£6
Well Dressing	£3	
Wheelwrights	£5–£10	

Superb examples will always fetch considerably more, over £20 not being unusual.

SCOUTS

Baden-Powell £5
   Early Military . . . . £10–£15
Boy Scout Groups
   Identified £5
   Unidentified . . . . 75+
Events . . . . £4–£6
H.Q. Official cards . . . . £4+
Jamborees . . . . £5–£25*
Personalities . . . . £3–£5
   Jack Cornwall £5
Activities, printed series . . . . . . £4+
   Photographic identified . . . £4–£6
   Comics . . . . £3–£5
Boys Brigade . . . . £2.50+
Girl Guides
   Lady Baden-Powell £4
   Princess Royal £2.50
   Princess Elizabeth . . . . £3+
   Other Leaders . . . . £2+
Camp Sites
   Official Cards £2.50
   Groups . . . . 75–£1.50
Other Youth Organisations . . . . . £1+

Used with special pmk adds considerably to the value. Sets usually command a premium.

Nº 5.

A SCOUT IS COURTEOUS

One of a rare series of 12 published in 1929 £5

REINTERMENT II PRIESTS GRANBY ROW 1820–45 TO MOSTON 1909   3

Re-interment – a jolly social history category. Anybody know why? £15

EXHIBITIONS

If a postcard has also an exhibition postmark this could increase the price considerably. The prices shown here are for the picture side only.

Nuremberg 1882	£35
Paris 1889	£25
Columbian 1893	£10
Berlin 1896	£10
Geneva 1896	£9
Nuremberg 1896	£9
Brussels 1897	£9
Hamburg 1897	£9
Leipzig 1897	£5
Turin 1898	£5
Paris 1900	£3
Glasgow 1901	£4
Pan-American 1901	£2
Cork 1902	£4
Wolverhampton 1902	£4
Earls Court 1903	£3
Highland 1903	£3
Bradford 1904	£4
Earls Court 1904	£2
Nantes 1904	50
Pan-Celtic Congress 1904	£1
St. Louis 1904	£1.50
Earls Court 1905	£1
Liege 1905	30
Nelson Centennial	50
I.R. Austrain 1906	75–£1.50
Marseilles 1906	25
Milan 1906	30
Irish International 1906	£1.50
Jamestown 1907	£1
Irish International 1907	£1.50
Liege 1907	30
Palestine Exhibition 1907	£2
Franco-British 1908	35
Franco-British Advertising	£5–£10
Franco-British Art Cards	£5–£10
Bradford Exhibition 1908	£2.50
Balkan States Exhibition 1908	75
Alaska-Yukon-Pacific 1909	75
Imperial International 1909	75
Brussels 1910	20
Canadian National 1910	75
Japan British 1910	35

Charleroi 1911	20
Coronation Exhibition 1911	75
Festival of Empire 1911	£1
Scottish 1911	£1
Turin 1911	20
Chromo-lithographs	£2.50
Vienna 1911	£15
Dusseldorf 1912	20
Latin British 1912	75
Ghent 1913	20
Leipzig 1913	20
Palestine Exhibition 1913	£1
Anglo-American 1914	40
Panama-Pacific 1915	50
Brussels-Leakin 1919	25
Marseilles 1922	20
British Empire 1924	50–£1+
Ernest Coffin Designs	£2
British Empire 1925	£1+

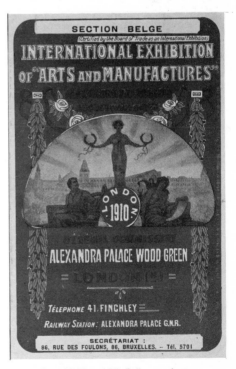

An exhibition at Ally Pally one of many miscellaneous exhibitions not listed £18

53

1938 Empire Exhibition pull-out advert £8

A view of the Festival of Britain £1.50

Paris 1925	40
Newcastle-upon-Tyne 1929	£3
Antwerp 1930	20
Liege 1930	20
Paris 1931	20
Brussels 1935	20
Paris 1937	20
Empire 1938	50
World's Fair 1939	30
Festival of Britain	75
Royle Publications Ltd	
watercolour views	£1.50
World's Fair 1960	30

Pageants

Bath (photo type)	75
(coloured type)	£1
Bradford	£1.50

Bury St. Edmunds	£1.50
Chelsea Historical	75
Colchester	£1
Coventry	75
Gloucester	£1
Liverpool	£1.50
National Pageant of Wales	£1
Newcastle-on-Tyne	£1.50
Oxford	75
River Peace	50
St. Albans (sepia)	75
(coloured)	£1.25
Warwick (photo)	60
(coloured)	£1
Winchester	75
Pageant Queens	50
Other type	40

FANTASY

Fantasy Heads B/W	£8–£15
Coloured	£30
Faces in Flowers	£3–£10
Faces in Mountains	
Killinger	£15–£25
Later Issues	£10–£15
Faces in Smoke, etc.	£2–£5
Babies/Children	£2–£3
Babies/Children Embossed	£5
Enlarged Objects	£1–£2
Erotic	£5–£15
Maps	£10–£15

Illustrations

Above right: An unusual Bulldog Henry VIII £10

Below left: A comic map of England £15

Below right: Mad Ludwig and one of his Castles on a Killinger mountain £16

Gruss aus Hamburg:

This type of framed view is very much collected. Greetings from Hamburg £3.50

Loving Birthday Greetings

There are so many beautiful embossed greetings cards; this one Tuck's Art Series 6842 £3.50

AUTOGRAPHS

Supplement by Derek Birch

The following are prices obtained for autographed postcards (based on autograph dealers, auctions, realisations, etc.)

Lilian Braithwaite £5

Bransby Williams – also an early TV Star £4

ACTORS/ACTRESSES

Yvonne Arnaud	£7
Leslie Banks	£5
Frank Benson	£5
Sarah Bernhardt	£25
Edna Best	£5
Lilian Braithwaite	£5
Mary Brough	£3
Marie Burke	£5
Herbert Campbell	£5
Mrs Patrick Campbell	£8
Fay Compton	£5
Gladys Cooper	£5
Cicely Courtneidge	£5
Adeline Genée	£5
Basil Gill	£3
Seymour Hicks	£3
Henry Irving	£12
R. G. Knowles	£7
Elsa Lanchester	£3
Lily Langtry	£20
Gertie Millar	£5
Walter Passmore	£5
Ada Reeve	£5
Rejane	£15
Arthur Roberts	£5
Alistair Sim	£15
Marie Tempest	£8
Ellen Terry	£12
Sybil Thorndike	£5
Tom Walls	£5
Williams, Bransby	£4
Charles Wyndham	£10
Most other actors/actresses	£1 upwards

MUSIC HALL

Maud Allen	£10
Arthur Askey	£2
Max Bacon	£2
Hylda Baker	£5
Wilkie Bard	£10
Fred Barnes	£2
Jack Benny	£10
Kitty Bluett	£3
Issy Bonn	£5
Teddy Brown	£15
Kate Carney	£5
Harry Champion	£7
Albert Chevelier	£5
Maurice Chevelier	£5
G. H. Chirgwin	£5
Charles Coburn	£5
Buffalo Bill Cody	£1
Tommy Cooper	£1
Whit Cunliffe	£5
Florence Desmond	£3
T. E. Dunville	£7
Gus Elen	£7
G. H. Elliott	£5
Fred Emney Snr	£7
Happy Fanny Fields	£5
Gracie Fields	£7
Flanagan & Allen	£10
George Formby	£7
Ronald Frankau	£5
Will Fyffe	£7
Gert & Daisy	£4
Gertie Gitana	£4
Grock (clown)	£10
Tony Hancock	£7
Tommy Handley	£6
Will Hay	£12
Bobby Howes	£4
Harry Houdini	£50
Roy Hudd	£1
Jimmy James	£5
Marie Kendall	£3
Hetty King	£8
Charles Kunz	£5
Lupino Lane	£5
Sir Harry Lauder	£10
Laurel & Hardy	£60
Millie Legarde	£3
Dan Leno	£20
Little Tich	£10

Marie Lloyd	£20
Cissie Loftus	£4
Max Miller	£10
Tessie O'Shea	£2
Vic Oliver	£2
Donald Peers	£3
Wilfred Pickles	£3
Sandy Powell	£5
George Robey	£7
Stainless Stephen	£2
Eugene Stratton	£12
Randolph Sutton	£5
Suzette Tarry	£4
Vesta Tilley	£5
Tommy Trinder	£4
Sophie Tucker	£4
Dicky Valentine	£4
Nellie Wallace	£5
Western Brothers	£2
Wee Georgie Wood	£4
Others	£1–£2

Harry Houdini – without chains! £50

Mr 'Wakey-Wakey' himself £5

A. J. Balfour £12

MUSICIANS, SINGERS & BALLET STARS

Sir John Barbaroli	£10
The Beatles	£40
Sir Thomas Beecham	£7
Jack Buchanan	£5
Eddie Calvert	£3
E. Caruso	£70
Noël Coward	£15
Dance Band Leaders	£2–£5
Anton Dolin	£2
E. Elgar	£40
Benjamin Gigli	£10
Dame Myra Hess	£5
Jan Kubelik	£5
Vera Lynn	£3
Alicia Markova	£4
Dame Nellie Melba	£20
Ivor Novello	£7
Sir Ch. Parry	£10
A. Patti	£30
Anna Pavlova	£50
Elvis Presley	£35
G. Puccini	£120
Leff Pouishnoff	£7
Paul Robeson	£20
Albert Sammons	£4
Sir Malcolm Sargent	£5
The Rolling Stones	£20
Richard Tauber	£10
L. Tetrazzini	£25
Sir Henry Wood	£8
Others	£3

POLITICIANS

H. H. Asquith	£12
A. J. Balfour	£12
Campbell Bannerman	£12
J. Chamberlain	£3
Lord George Brown	£1.50
Winston Churchill	£100
Lloyd George	£12
Keir Hardie	£7
Lansdowne	£3
H. Bonar Law	£12
Harold Wilson	£2
Other Cabinet Ministers	£2

EXPLORER
Sir Ernest Shackleton £20

AUTHORS
W. H. Auden £14
J. M. Barrie £18
Hilaire Belloc £18
G. K. Chesterton £30
J. Galsworthy £20
Aldous Huxley £25
Jerome K. Jerome £15
Rudyard Kipling £18
Oliver Lodge £10
Margaret Mitchell £10
Baroness D'Orczy . . . . £20+
A. Pinero £6
Ezra Pound £25
G. B. Shaw . . . . £30+
Leo Tolstoy £80
H. G. Wells £12
P. G. Wodehouse £10
Virginia Woolf £130

Jerome K. Jerome £15

Sir Arthur Conan Doyle (not listed here). Perhaps Holmes can find a price!

SPORTSMEN
Max Baer £5
Henry Cooper £3
J. Davis £12
Jack Dempsey £7
W. G. Grace £40
J. Hobbs £7
Cricketers of 30s–50s . . . . . £3+
Tennis Players £6

MILITARY
Lord Baden Powell £30
Redvers Buller £15
Sir John French £15
Kitchener £15
Montgomery of Alamein £40
Lord Roberts £15

SUFFRAGETTES
Christabel Pankhurst £25
Others £10

J. B. Gilbert at Wimbledon £6

FILM STARS

Many film star postcards have signatures *printed* in blue ink. These are *not* eligible as autographed postcards.

Joan Crawford	£10
Deanna Durbin	£5
Laurel & Hardy	£60
Vivien Leigh	£20

No section for postcard artists yet, but who could resist a signed 'Bonzo' from the editor's collection.

Sabu	£20
Alistair Sim	£10
C. Aubrey Smith	£8
Shirley Temple	£10
John Wayne	£25
Most Hollywood Stars of 30s	£5 upwards

ROYALTY

Queen Alexandra	£30
Edward VIII	£50
George VI	£50
Queen Mary	£15

Votes for Women.

Madame AINO MALMBERG.

Published by the Women's Freedom League, *1, Robert Street, Adelphi, W.C.*

Women's Suffrage. £10 for signature – but must be worth £15 on official card

Amendments To
COLOURED COMMERCIAL RAILWAY CARD SUPPLEMENT 1982
Pages S1–S42

There have been no major discoveries since the 1982 supplement was published, but there were a few errors and omissions. Thanks are due to a number of people who have written in with comments and corrections, particularly Norman Kerr and Hardy Lee. These amendments have been prepared by John Alsop.

Page S2   H.M. & Co.

This series by H. Moss was numbered 4256, and there is also a French printing by K. F. Editeurs. Spelling of place names varies, e.g. 23 has Galatz or Galicia.

Add   **25** Switzerland. The Gotthard Express.
         26 Russia. St Petersburgh–Moscow. (V)
         27 United States. Central Pacific New York–St. Francisco.
         28 The Flying Scotchman.
         29 Italy. Genoa–Rome.
         30 Netherlands. Amsterdam–Rotterdam.
         31 Belgium. Brussels–Ostend.

Page S4   HIGH LEVEL SERIES
This series was by Hills of Sunderland.

Page S5   HOMEWOOD OF BURGESS HILL
Add   **91A** From the Level Crossing, Burgess Hill.

Pages S10–S18   LOCOMOTIVE PUBLISHING COMPANY
A number of additional Alpha reprints have been reported. Some of these have no series number; these are shown as Alpha. There are a few corrections to other reprints, and the notes on reprints 1–120 say 73–78 do not exist. It now seems that 75 and 78 do exist, but 55 and 79 do not, so the old stock was used for numbers 55, 73, 74, 76, 77, 79.

Add					
173 A1403		**261** A1303		**358** Alpha	
183 A1303		**262** Alpha		**371** A1417	
192 A1405		**269** Alpha		**380** A1409	
193 A1303		**283** A1404		**406** A1302	
247 Alpha		**327** A1402		**418** Alpha	

Amend   **194** and **200** Delete?
         214 R28 not R98
         265 R78 not R79
         282 R75 not R55
Add   **308** R1
Amend   Move all reprints shown against 311–316 down one line to 312–317.

MONARCH

There are a number of collotype cards, some of which are known hand tinted, dating from c.1904. It is hoped that it will be possible to list these some time in the future.

Pages S27–S28 **RUSSELLS and SCOTT RUSSELL**

These two publishers were almost certainly the same company, which is known to have changed names several times.

SALMON

Some variations, and 9 cards were inadvertently omitted. There were at least three issues of 565–570:

> Untitled
>
> Title on picture
>
> and a printing by W. Mack.

571–576 were reprinted post-grouping with amended titles.

Add **592A** 4383 The Automotrice Bugatti P.L.M.

592B 4384 Commodore Vanderbilt, New York Central Rly.

592C 4385 The Flying Hamburger, German State Rlys.

599A 4976 G.W.R. Express Locomotive 'Viscount Portal'

599B 4977 S.R. Express Locomotive 'Lord Nelson'

599C 4978 S.R. Express Locomotive 'Salisbury'

599D 4979 L.M.S. Express Locomotive 'City of Leicester'

599E 4980 L.N.E.R. Express Locomotive 'Dwight D. Eisenhower'

599F 4981 L.N.E.R. Express Locomotive 'Edward Thompson'

TUCK

Page S30 Series 6493 was issued by September 1904.

Series 9150 was reprinted post-grouping, omitting 633, the set being made up with 627 from Series 9040.

Page S33 Series 9972 was out by March 1916.

Page S34 If the backs of the cards are to be believed, there are some unexpected railway artists. 727 and 731 are attributed to Jennie Harbour and 732 to Ned Sherrin.

AN UNLISTED HARRY PAYNE

Cat No 537A

Tuck 'Celebrated Posters' Series 1508 for Scottish Tyres is revealed as an unlisted Harry Payne dated /92. This is the only known Harry Payne postcard with a dated signature. The card is used in November 1904 and according to the message on the back was obtained at the Stanley Cycle Show (Perthshire?). Value £75.

GREETINGS

FATHER CHRISTMAS
Early embossed
  (red robes) £6
  (other colour robes) £8
Non-embossed £3
Photo type . . . . 75+
First World War Silk types *see Silk Section*
Hold to Light type *see under Novelty*

GREETINGS TYPES
Birthday – Deckle-edge *c.*1930 . . . 10
  Other types 10
Christmas 15
Decoration Day . . . . £4–£5
Easter 30
Halloween £2
Jewish New Year . . . . £3–£5
New Year 20
St. Patrick's Day £3
Thanksgiving Day £3

**A delightful Valentine
in Tuck 'Remembrance' Series R1033 £4**

Valentine's Day . . . . £2–£5
Embossed – early £3
  Other types . . . . 30+
Faith, Hope & Charity
  Set of . . . . £3–£6+
  Single cards . . . . 50–£3
Hands across the Sea . . . . . 50–£2
Independence Day £4
Illuminations 20
Maps (romantic & comic) 30
Moonlight . . . . 25+
Mottoes/Sayings 30
Rough Seas . . . . 20+
Silhouettes . . . . 75+
Silks (embroidered & woven)
  see under Silks
Sunsets 10
Swastikas/Greetings type 30
Twenty-First Birthday 20
Wedding Anniversary 20
Wedding Day 20

**Swimming at Christmas! Must be 'Down Under'.
This one about £2**

Early Inter-Art Pub. Co. embossed Christmas card £3

PUBLISHERS OF GREETINGS POSTCARDS

We feel that the diversity of most publishers' work makes nonsense of any attempt to quote a price for their cards, except where they fall into other listed categories.

LARGE LETTER

Date cards (embossed type)	£3
Year cards (embossed type)	£4–£6
Calendar cards	£2
Days of the week	50
Initials/Alphabet	75–£1.50
Initials, Tuck's 'Cherubs'	£5
Initials, Complete Sets	£35–£150
Names of boys	40+
Names of girls	30+
Names of places	£1+
Numbers	50–£1.50

Hold to Light *see under Novelty*

LANGUAGE OF . . .

Flowers (Welch, J.)	75
Others	50+
Fruit	50
Stamps	£2
Vegetables (Valentine series)	50
Other issues	50

Embossed year date card with New Year Greeting on reverse £4

HERALDIC

Prices quoted are for Town names, other types exist i.e. Counties, Colleges, Houses, which are worth less, overseas countries, more.

Tuck's 'Heraldic' early	£6
B. & R.'s Camera Series	£1
E.F.A. Series	£1.25
Faulkner, C.W.	£1
Early	£6
F.S.O. Heraldic Series	£1.25
Ja-Ja Series	£1.25
Jarrold's Series	£1+
Rapid Photo Printing Co.	75
Valentine's	75
W.E.B.	75
W.R. & S. Reliable Series	75
Miscellaneous	75–£1

TARTANS

B.B. Tartan view series	50+
B. & R.'s (Arms, Views & Tartans)	50
B. & R.'s Camera series	35

This type of superb early heraldic card is also, of course, a greetings card £6

Cynicus Co. Tartans	75
Davinson's Scotch, Design series	40
Hartmann, The Clans of Scotland	75
Ja-Ja Series	£1
Greetings Tartan design	30
Johnston, W. & A.K.	
Tartan & Arms Series	75
Others	20
N.B.'s series (Families)	50
Newman Brothers (View & Tartans)	30
Philco series (Views & Tartans)	50
Ross series	30
Tuck, R. & Sons, Scottish Clans	£1.50
Schwerdtfeger, E.A. & Co.	
(Tartans, Views and Verse)	25
W. & K. Series (Badge & Tartan)	£1
Valentine's Tartan Series	50
Other types	25

Early Faulkner 'Coats of Arms' Series 53 £6

THE CLOG SHOP, N.C.H.O. EDGWORTH.

ST. CRISPIN CRAFT.

Hot workers of the old time styled
The GENTLE CRAFT of LEATHER,
Young brothers of the ancient Guild,
Stand forth once more together;
The foot is yours, where'er it falls,
It treads your well-wrought leather,
On earthen floor, in marble halls,
On carpet or on heather,

The red brick to the mason's hand,
The brown earth to the tiller's;
The shoe is yours, shall wealth command,
Like fairy Cinderella's;
As they who shunned the household maid
Beheld the crown upon her,
So all shall see your toil repaid
With wealth and home and honour.

Two superb printed cards showing the clog makers at the N.C.H.O., Edgworth, nr Bolton.
£10 for the pair. How much if photographic?

PORTION OF CLOG SHOP, N.C.H.O. EDGWORTH.

INDUSTRIAL

Prices for these categories vary considerably according to area – some being more sought after than others – and photographic cards are considered better than printed.

COAL MINING

Coal Miners – Groups, identified	£4+
Single	£2
Coal Mines	£4–£8
Pithead	£4–£6
Coal Mine Disasters	£6–£8
Memorium Cards	£10+
Memorium Gothard	£15–£25
Coal Mining – Art	£1
Exhibitions	75
Wenches	£2–£4
Sinking New Colliery	£8
Colliery Railway Engines	£2+
Royal Visits	£4–£6
Strikes (Black Leg Marches)	£15+
Coal Ships	£2
Colliery Model Postcards	£1
Miner's Song & Poem (Sets)	£1–£3

Quarrying – Crawfordjohn, Lanarkshire £6

Underground Views	£4
(Artist Type)	£1.50
Miners' Funerals	£6–£8
Mine Rescue Teams	£4–£6

INDUSTRIAL

Blast Furnace	£2–£3
Boat Repairs	£3
Factories	£3
Machine Shops	£2–£4
Mills	
Cotton (interior)	£2–£3
Iron	£2–£3
Steel	£2–£3
Woollen	£2–£3
Mining	
Copper	£1.50
Gold	£1.50
Iron	£2–£6
Tin	£3–£10
Power Houses	£2–£3
Printing Works	£2–£3
Royal Mint	40

Maltby Colliery, Yorkshire £5

Dickens' characters Tuck Series 3407
by Harold Copping £2.50

Shakespeare's children a Faulkner Series
by Cicely Mary Barker £2.50

Abraham's of Keswick produced this beautiful
portrait series of Lakeland Literary figures £1

Early Tuck 'Art' of Sir Walter Scott's
'Young Lochivar' artist J. Finnemore £6

LITERARY & MUSIC

LITERARY

Dickens early numbered	
Tuck, R.	£8
Dickens Postcard Series	
Tuck, R. 'Kyd'	£6+
Dickens Characters	
Tuck, R.	£2.50
In Dickens Land Tuck, R. Scenes	£2
Views	£1.25
Dickens Sketches	75
Dickens Houses	20
Alice in Wonderland	£1–£3
Lorna Doone Series	75
Poetry (Patience Strong Series)	40
Poetry (Burns)	25
Poetry (Others)	30
Shakespeare	
Tuck, R. Early	£8
Oilette	£1
Portraits	30
Ernest Lister	
Chromo-litho Scenes	£4

Widmung (von Schumann)

Dass du mich liebst
Macht mich mir werth
Dein Blick hat mich vor mir verklärt
Du hebst mich liebend über mich
Mein guter Geist, mein bess'res Ich.

Beautiful embossed chromolitho with verse from Schumann's songs £3

C. W. Faulkner Series	£4
Hildesheimer Series	£1.50–£2.50

MUSIC

Bands – Dance (known)	£3
Jazz (known)	£5
Brass	£1.50
Military	£1.50+
Bandstands	30+
Bells identified local	£3+
Bell Ringers identified groups	£4+
Champion Bandsmen	£1
Composers Art	£1–£5
Photo	50–75
Dagenham Girl Pipers	40
Gramophones	£1–£2
Comic Type	£1.50+
Hymns	40
Musical Instruments	20

H. J. Wood,
Conductor of the Queens Hall Orchestra.

First of the Promenaders £3

Opera
  Gilbert & Sullivan
    D'Oyley Carte Opera Co
      Parkslee Pictures £2
      G & S Photos 75
      Savoyard Photos 75
      Amateur Performances £1
    Sir Thomas Beecham
      Opera Co (Rotary) £1.50
    Clara Butt 75
    Caruso £3
    Melba £2.50
  Orchestras 60
  Organs – Church (close-up) . . . . £1+
  Other types (close-up) £2
  Rotary Photo Series Music and
    Composers 40
  Singers 40
    Jazz £4

An unusual Ethel Parkinson song card £3

SONG CARDS
Bamforth Postcards
Song & Hymn Cards
  In sets of 3 . . . . £1.50
  In sets of 4 . . . . £2
Odd cards 50
Black and white odds 50

Other Publishers
Davidson Bros. 35
H.G.L. 35
Photochrom Co. Ltd 25
Inter-Art Co. 35
Philco Pub. Co. 35
Rapid Photo Co. 35
Rotary Series 20
Tuck, R. & Sons
  (Illustrated Song Series) £1
Valentine's Series 35

He kept them spellbound! Parkslee Pictures £2

MILITARY

SPANISH AMERICAN WAR 1898 . £4–£6
BOER WAR
Souvenir of 1900 (Tuck, R. & Sons) . £15
Peace Card, coloured
   (Tuck, R. & Sons) £15
Tuck, R. & Sons 'Empire'
   Coloured £15
   B/W . . . . £8–£12
Ships . . . . £10–£12
Early Vignettes – Coloured . . . £12–£15
   Black/white . . . . £8–£12
Overprinted for Victories £25
C.I.V. – B/W Vignettes (City Press) . . £8
War Sketches £8
European Cards (views) . . . . . £6–£8
Cartoons Black/white £10
   Coloured . . . . £10–£15
War Photographs £10
BOXER REBELLION 1900
War Photographs £5
Cartoons, coloured £15

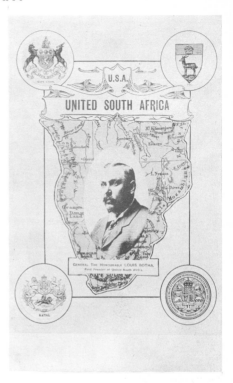

**Right: To commemorate the Union.
The message reads '. . . Hope you like this
photo of an old Dutch Farmer' £8**

**Below: South African War postcard No 2
published by Geo Stewart & Co £10**

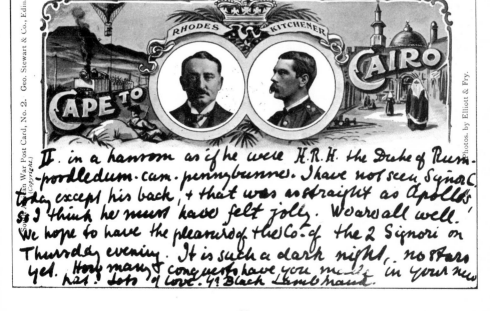

RUSSO-JAPANESE WAR 1905

War Photographs
   (Government issued) £4
War Photographs (others) £2.50
War Sketches
   (War Series/Hildesheimer, S.) . . £1.50
War Sketches . . . . £2–£4

CHINESE CIVIL WAR 1912

War Photographs £3

WORLD WAR 1

Allied Occupation, Germany 1919 . . 75
Campaign Maps . . . . £2+
Cemeteries 10
Christmas Cards £1.50
   (From POW etc. Camps) . . . £5–£10
Dardanelles Campaign 50
Mesopotamia Campaign 50
Memorials . . . . 30+
Palestine Campaign £1.50
Recruiting Posters £25
Salonika Campaign 20
Shell Damage, G.B. . . . . £1.50–£2.50

British buses at the Front advertising Dubonnet £8

Tanks
   British . . . . 75–£1.50
   Foreign . . . . 75–£1.50
War Bond Campaign
   Trafalgar Square £1.50
   Local Visits . . . . £6–£8
Victory Parade, London . . . . . 50–£1
   Foreign 30
   Local . . . . £3–£6
War Wounded . . . . 20+

Other Types

Allied German Camps (photo type) . £1
Allied German Camps (art type) . £3–£5+
German Camps £1
Lord Kitchener £1.25
   Memorial Cards £2.50
Other Military Persons
   Gt. Britain . . . . 75+
   German 50
   French 40
   Other Countries 40
Military Art Type Postcards
   (except listed artists) . . . . £1–£2.50

Russo-Japanese War (Embossed) £6

Miscellaneous

Army Camps, Fields (identified)	£1.50
Huts	£1.50
Barracks	£1.50
General scenes	75+
Artillery	40
Beefeaters	20
British in India	40
History & Traditions (Gale & Polden)	£3.50
Rates of Pay cards	£15+
Regimental Badges (G & P)	£2+

(remainders of some of these have been found)

Life in the Army (Gale & Polden)	£1.50
Life in the Army (Star Series)	50
Life in the Army (other types)	£1
Medals, Rees, H.	
(Present Day War Ribbons)	£3
Daring Deeds	£2–£3
V.C. Winners	£2–£5
Military Art Types Col.	£1.50–£2.50
Sepia & B/W	50–£1

One of the Gale & Polden's Portrait
'History & Traditions' £3.50

Military Tattoos (Aldershot)	50
Royal Tournament	75
Others	75
Regimental Photographs	50
Special Interest (visits, etc.)	£1.50+
Belgian Relief Fund	50
British Ambulance Committee	50
British Committee of the French Red Cross	£1
British Gifts for Belgian Soldiers	50

War Photographs/Sketches

Daily Mail (Battle Pictures)	75+
Daily Mirror	50
Imperial War Museum	30
Regent Publishing Co.	
The War Series	50
Sketch, The	50
Sphere, The	75

A Second World War cartoon by A. Jaegy £12

PATRIOTIC

Art type	£1.50–£3.50
Boer War *see above*	
Bull Dogs	£1.50
Comic type	£1.50–£2.50
Greetings type	50–£1
Flags	£1.50
Nelson type	50
Poem type	75
Punch (issued by)	£1
Royalty type	£1–£2.50
Romantic type	50+
Soldier's verse	50–75
Thanksgiving	50–£1

SPANISH CIVIL WAR 1935 . . . . £10+

ABYSSINIAN WAR 1939 . . . . . £4–£6

A patriotic birthday greeting £1.50

WORLD WAR II

Germany, Nazi issues	£4–£10
Great Britain, Bomb Damage	£1.50+
Comic	£2.50
Leaders	£1–£2
Churchill	£2–£4
Netherlands,	
Cartoons, Anti-Nazi	£6
Comics	£2.50
Leaders (Allied)	£1–£2
U.S.A., Comic and Patriotic	75–£1.50

MILITARY ARTISTS

Bairnsfather, B.	£1.50
Baker, Granville H.	£3
Becker, C.	£6
Beraud, N.	£3
Bourillon	£2
Chidley, Arthur	£2.50
Cremieux, Suzanne	
(Croix de Guerre des Allies)	£5
Dupuis, Emil	£4
Hardy, F.C.	£1.50
Henclke, Carl	£4
Holloway, Edgar A.	£2.50
Hudson, Gerald	£2
Ibbetson, Ernest	£3
Leigh, Conrad	50
McNeill, J.	£2
O'Bierne, F.	£8+
Payne, Harry	
Tuck's Early	£8–£25
Oilette	£2–£15
Badges & Wearers	£6–£15
Stewart & Woolfe	£8
Gale & Polden	£6–£8

See 1981 Editions for full listing and 1982 for Amendments.

Simkin, R.	£8
Stewart, J.A.	£2.50
Toussaint, M.	£6
Ward, Herbert	£2.50
Woodville, R. Caton	£2.50

NOVELTY

APPLIQUÉ TYPES

Dried Flowers £1
Feathered Birds (real feathers) . £6–£10
Feathered Hats £4
Jewels . . . . £1+
Metal Models (cars, etc.) £2.50
Real Hair . . . . £6–£8
Sandpaper (match strikers) £4
Sand Pictures £2
Sand Pictures (Isle of Wight) £3
Velvet £1.50
Other types 75

COIN

National (embossed) £6
National (printed) £5
Coin Greetings type £3
Banknotes . . . . £4–£6

KEEP ME AS A MASCOT PROPER
AN' YOU'LL NEVER LACK A COPPER!

**A Mabel Lucie Attwell 'stand up' cut-out card
at least £8**

This must be unique – the insert at the bottom is a
mouth organ –and it works £25?

COMPOSITE SETS

Large 10–12 cards (Napoleon, Christ,
    Jean d'Arc, etc) . . . . £40–£60
Early European Sets 3–5 cards
    (usually animals) . . . . . . £30–£50
American Sets . . . . £20–£50
G.P. Govt. Tea (Edward VII) £120

HOLD-TO-LIGHT

Continental £6
Exhibitions £6
G.B. Views (cut out type) . . . . . £3+
Greetings (Father Xmas) . . . . . £25+
Greetings (Others) £5

MECHANICAL TYPES

Blow out type	£8
Kaleidoscopes	£15–£25
Lever change type	£3
Moveable hats	£3
Paper chains	£10–£15
Venetian blinds	£3
Roller blinds (early)	£30
Rotating types	£5–£10
Stand up types	£5
Other types	£1.50

PULL-OUT TYPES

(usually with town names & views)

Animals (wild)	£1–£1.50
Artist (Mabel Lucie Attwell, etc.)	£2
Bottles of beer	£2.50
Bus	£2.50
Cars (motor)	£2
Cats	£1.50
Comic	£1.50
Coronation Souvenir	£3
Dogs	£1.50
Fortune Telling	£2
Irish Shamrocks, etc.	£2
Maps	£2.50
Military type, Camps	£2
Soldiers	£1.50
Other	£1.50
Postman	£2–£3
Products (tins of salmon, etc.)	£1.50
Railway Tickets (town names)	£1.50
Rural Scenes	
(Kent hop fields, etc.)	£4–£6
Ships	£1.50
Trams	£3
Valentine (Heraldic type)	£1.50
Views of towns (multi-view fronts)	£1.50
Welsh Ladies	£1–£2

STAMP CARDS

Embossed (Zieher, O.)	£6
USA (Zieher, O.)	£10
(other publishers)	£5
Printed (Zieher, O.)	£5
Other Publishers	£4+
Black & White Printed	£2+
Modern (Robson Lowe Ltd)	50

TRANSPARENCIES

Continental	£10
Exhibitions	£10–£15
G.B. views (col. change)	£3
G.B. views Meteor Type. published	
by Hartmann	£8
Greetings (Father Xmas)	£8
(Others)	£4–£6
Meteors	£10
Puzzle type	£4

MISCELLANEOUS

Aluminium	£2.50
Bas Relief	£1
Bookmark types	75+
Celluloid	£2
embossed (very rare)	£6
Cut out models Tuck, W. E. Mack,	
Jas Henderson, etc.	£12–£30
Later Issues (Salmon)	£3+
Glass eyes (cats, etc.)	£2
Glitter type	30
Gramophone Records (Tuck, R.)	£4
(Early type)	£10
(Other types)	£5
Invisible picture type (coin rub, etc.)	£3
Jigsaw puzzles (Tuck, R.)	£12
(Other types)	£10
Leather	£3
Midget type	75
Mirror type	£1
Panel type	30
Peat type (real Irish)	£3
Perfumed	£1.50
Photo inset – seaside	50
Puzzle type	£2
Shapes	£2–£10
Squeakers	£2+
Stereoscopic (Magic Postcard)	£4
3D types (complete with eye-piece)	£4
Unusual sizes (all other than listed)	£1
Wood	£2

OVERSEAS

We have pitched the prices at the level you would expect to pay from a dealer who had a market for this type of card, but not the specialist buyers, mainly philatelic, who exist and would, in some cases, pay more.

European cards: prices given are for G.B. market and for further information see appropriate overseas catalogues in Bibliography.

Aden*	50
Algeria	30
Antigua*	£1.50
Argentina	40
Ascension**	£6
Austria	50–£1
Australia (street scenes)	£1+
(Others)	40+
Art cards see under Artists	
Bahamas	£1
(American coloured type)	60
Barbados*	£1
Basutoland*	£1
Belgium Streets and Villages . . .	£1–£2
Bermuda*	£1
Bolivia	60
Brazil	60
British Guiana	75
British Honduras	£1.50
Bulgaria	60
Burma	60
Canada – Patriotic (embossed) . .	£4–£6
Souvenir	£1.50+
Street Scenes	50–£1
Ceylon	40
Chile	60
China*	40
Colombia	40
Crete**	60+
Cuba	40
Cyprus*	£1+
Czechoslavakia	40
Danish W. Indies*	£1
Denmark (Streets)	75+
Dominica*	£1
Egypt	30
Equador	50
Estonia	60

A Baby Sperm Whale. Bermuda.

Bermuda an interesting card £1

Falkland Islands** £10
   Penguins and Birds** £5
Fiji* £1
Finland (Street Scenes) . . . . . £1+
France (Street Scenes) . . . . 75–£1.50
French Colonies* . . . . 20–£1
Germany . . . . 50–£1
Gibraltar* 40
Gilbert and Ellice Islands** £5
Greece . . . . £1+
Grenada (G.B. Colony)* £1
Hong Kong* 75
Hungary 50
Iceland . . . . £1+
India 30
Iraq 60
Italy 50
Jamaica* . . . . 75+
Japan 30
Labuan** £3
Lagos* 75
Latvia 75

A costume from Greece £1

Douches à l'Établissement Thermal d'Aix-les-Bains.
G. Brun, phot. édit., Aix (Savoie).

A thermal bath in France £3

Lebanon 75
Leeward Islands* £1
Lithuania 75
Malaya 75
Malta* 40
Mauritius* . . . . 75+
Mexico 50
Montenegro 60
Montserrat* (G.B. Colony) £1
Morocco* 40
Netherlands . . . . £1–£2
   Street Scenes and Villages . . . £1–£3
New Guinea* £2
New Hebrides* £2
New Zealand . . . . 50–£1
Nigeria . . . . 50+
Norfolk Islands** £5
North Borneo* · £3
Norway . . . . 30–£1
Palestine* . . . . 50+
Panama 40
Papua* £2

```
Persia  . . . . . . . . . . . . 75
Pitcairn Island**  . . . . . . . . £5
Poland  . . . . . . . . . . . . 50
Portugal  . . . . . . . . . . . 50
Rhodesia*  . . . . . . . . . . . £1+
Romania  . . . . . . . . . . . 50
Russia*  . . . . . . . . . . . . 50–£1
St. Helena*  . . . . . . . . . . £1.50
St. Kitts*  . . . . . . . . . . . £1
St. Lucia*  . . . . . . . . . . . £1
St. Vincent*  . . . . . . . . . . £4
Samoa*  . . . . . . . . . . . . £2
Sarawak*  . . . . . . . . . . . £3
Serbia  . . . . . . . . . . . . 60
Seychelles*  . . . . . . . . . . £5
Sierra Leone  . . . . . . . . . 50
Solomon Islands**  . . . . . . . . £3
South Africa  . . . . . . . . . 75–£2
```

Seychelles,
Lighthouse, Denis Island.

A good lighthouse on Seychelles £5

```
Spain  . . . . . . . . . . . . . 50
Sudan*  . . . . . . . . . . . . 60
Sweden  . . . . . . . . . . . . 50–£1
Switzerland  . . . . . . . . . . 25–50
Syria  . . . . . . . . . . . . . 75
Thailand*  . . . . . . . . . . . £1
Tonga*  . . . . . . . . . . . . £2
Trinidad*  . . . . . . . . . . . £1
Turkey*  . . . . . . . . . . . . 40
Uganda*  . . . . . . . . . . . . 75
U.S.A.  . . . . . . . . . . . . 50–£1
Yugoslavia  . . . . . . . . . . 50
Zanzibar*  . . . . . . . . . . . 75–£1
```

*Indicates that, if postally used in the place
of origin they are possibly worth more.
Indicates **definitely worth much more.

A carib stone from St Vincent £4

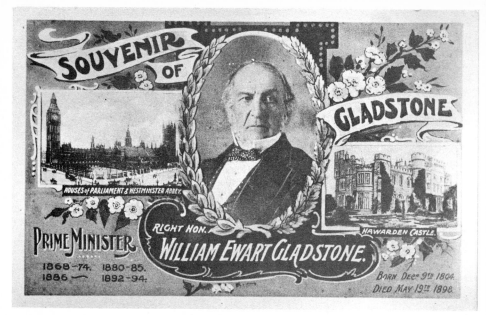

Souvenir of a great Prime Minister £3.50

"ST. GEORGE"
AND THE DRAGON

Lloyd George was the butt of many political cartoonists. This one anonymous £3.50

POLITICAL

CARTOONS

Dreyfus 1899	£8+
Alsace Lorraine 1903	£6
Bulgaria 1903	£6
Irish Home Rule 1912	£12

see also Military Section

World War 1 1914–1918

Edith Cavell – Mourning Cards . . .	£2
France (Les Monstres des Cathédrales)	£4
France (other issues)	£1.50
Germany	£2.50
Great Britain (Jarrold & Sons Punch Reproductions)	£1.50
Great Britain, Tuck, R. & Sons (Aesop's Fables)	£6
Great Britain	£1.50
Italy (sculpture montage)	£2

A card published by the Tariff Reform League – a much debated subject £3.50

Italy	£1.50
Human Butterflies (Pretty Girls/ Statesmen)	£6
Raemaeker, Louis	£1.50
Other issues	£1.50
World War II	£3–£5

SOCIAL CARTOONS

R. Tuck & Sons Political Postcards (early) . . .	£12–£15
Fiscal Series PVB	£5
Fiscal Series Others	£3.50
J. Walker & Co., Harry Furniss	£4
Davidson Bros., A. Ludovici	£3
Free Trade	£3–£5
Worker's Compensation Acts	£3
Suffragette Campaigns	£6–£8
National Insurance Acts	£3–£4
Shops Acts	£3
Irish Home Rule	£12

The Suffragette was active in the States too! £10

GENERAL

Dreyfus Affair . . . . £8–£12

Elections

Canvassing Cards . . . . £3+

Declarations . . . . £4–£6

Events

Meetings/Treaties . . . . £2–£3

Funerals . . . . £2+

Visits . . . . £2–£4

Irish Home Rule

Easter Rising 1916 . . . . £4+

   Leaders £8

   Mourning Cards . . . . £12+

Ulster Campaign £10

National Socialist Party . . . . . £4–£10

Personalities

Churchill . . . . £2–£5

Leaders/Statesmen . . . . . . £1–£3

Suffragette Campaigns

Events . . . . £8–£12

Publicity Cards . . . . £10–£15

Leaders/Portraits £12

Unrest

Evictions . . . . £15–£25

Marches and Strikes . . . . . . £5–£25

Sydney Street Siege, 1912 . . . . . £3+

There's nothing new!
Student damage in Bristol 1913 £15

A Ludovici cartoon published by Davidson Bros £3.50

POSTCARD INTEREST

PIONEER POSTCARDS
Official Stationery
Austria
First issue of postcard used
October 1st, 1869 . . . . £150
As above unused £10
Great Britain
First issue of postcard used
October 1st, 1870 . . . . £200
As above unused £4
Penny Postage Jubilee used 1890 . . £40
As above – unused £20
Royal Naval Exhibition (Eddystone
Lighthouse) used 1891 . . . . . . £40
Gardening & Forestry Exhibition
1893 – used £50
Austrian 25 years Jubilee Postcard showing
Dr. Hermann signed £250

GRUSS AUS FOREIGN
Vignette Views
Coloured used . . . . £2+
Mint . . . . £4+
B/W £1.50

Used in
1898 . . . . £3
1897 . . . . £4
1896 . . . . £5

1895 . . . . £6
1894 . . . . £8
1893 . . . . £10
1892 . . . . £12
1891 . . . . £15
1890 . . . . £20
Pre-1890 . . . . £25–£50

Anniversaries . . . . £10–£15
Exhibitions . . . . £10–£15
Festivals £10
Parades . . . . £10–£15
Souvenirs . . . . £8–£15
German Colonies . . . . £5–£10

GREAT BRITAIN EARLY

Court Sized
Gruss Aus type £15
British Colonies £10
Vignettes Coloured . . . . . £10–£15
Black/white . . . . £6+

Used in
1898 . . . . £8
1897 . . . . £10
1896 . . . . £15+
1895 . . . . £25–£50
1894 . . . . £200+

1897 Queen Victoria Jubilee Card £75

Early Italian vignette £6

Used cards may be proved as to year by the dated postmark on the Victorian Stamp but the presence of a Victorian Stamp with an indecipherable date is NOT proof that it is pre-1902 because Victorian Stamps were regularly used in 1902, then decreasingly for a year or so later and freak usage is found many years later. As regards UNUSED cards, they are more difficult to allocate to their year and the ability to date can come only with experience, save that 'Court' cards are usually associated with this pre-1902 period.

Intermediate Sized

Vignette Black/white	£8
Vignette Coloured	£10–£15

Normal Sized (up to 1902)

Gruss Aus type	£10
Vignette Coloured	£3–£6
Vignette Black/white	£1–£3

N.B. For used see p 77

POSTCARD EXHIBITIONS

1898–1899	£75–£150
1900–1920	£25–£50
1921–1974	£10–£25
Modern	£1–£5

MODERN POSTCARDS

The Editors feel that, as much as they admire some of the magnificent cards being produced today, the subject is outside the scope of this catalogue and to attempt to list them would require a catalogue of similar size to this.

Label for International Society of
Postcard Collectors 'Globe'.
Cannot put a value on these

Tuck advertising for British Industries Fair 1917.
At least £10 for this

OFFICIAL POST OFFICE PICTURE CARDS (P.H.Q.)

N.B. These issues are mainly collected by Stamp Collectors and therefore tend **to rise (and fall)** *with the stamp market. They must be in* **perfect** *condition.*

P.O.	Ref No		
1973	1	Cricket	£50
	2	I. Jones	£55
	3	Parliament	£30
	4	R. Wedding	£10
1974	5	Tree	£95
	6	Fire Service	£95
	7	Britons (4)	£11
	8	Churchill	£5
1975	9	Turner	£15
	10	Euro Arch (3)	£6
	11	Sailing	£4
	12	Railways (4)	£45
	13	Jane Austen (4)	£10
1976	14	Pioneers	£6
	15	Bicentennial	£4.50
	16	Roses (4)	£13
	17	Folk Activities (4)	£4
	18	Caxton (4)	£4
	19	Christmas (4)	£2.25
1977	20	Racket Sports (4) . . .	£4.50
	21	Chemistry (4)	£3.75
	22	S. Jubilee (5)	£8
	23	Heads of Govt.	£2
	24	Not Issued	
	25	Wildlife (5)	£2.25
	26	Christmas (6)	£2.25
1978	27	Energy (4)	£2.25
	28	Hist. Builds. (4)	£2.25
	29	Coronation (4)	£2
	30	Horses (4)	£2
	31	Cycling (4)	£1.25
	32	Christmas (4)	£1.25
1979	33	Dogs (4)	£1.50
	34	Flowers (4)	80
	35	Dir. Elects. (4)	£1.25
	36	Horse Racing (4)	75
	37	Year of Child (4)	75
	38	Rowland Hill (4)	75
	39	Police (4)	75
	40	Christmas (5)	£1.25
1980	41	Birds (4)	75
	42	Railway (5)	£1
	43	1980 Exhib.	30
	43	Landmarks (5)	£1
	44	Famous Women	80
	45	Queen Mother	35
	46	Music (4)	75
	47	Sport (4)	75
	48	Christmas (5)	85
1981	49	Folklore (4)	85
	50	Disabled (4)	85
	51	Butterflies (4)	85
	52	National Trust (4)	£1
	53	Royal Wedding (2) . . .	75
	54	Duke of Edinburgh (4) .	95
	55	Fishing (4)	95
	56	Christmas (5)	£1.25
1982	57	Darwin (4)	95
	58	Youth (4)	95
	59	Theatre (4)	95
	60	Maritime (5)	£1.25
	61	Textiles (4)	95

EXAMPLES OF NORTH STAFFORDSHIRE TYPES

A North Stafford Railway Correspondence
Card used in 1906 £10

The NSR produced 3 cards of Cauldon Low Cave,
later destroyed by quarrying operations £4

North Stafford Railway Set 5 £3

North Stafford Railway Set 11 £4

North Stafford Railway Set 15 £6

North Stafford Railway Set 17 £6

North Stafford Railway Set 19 £6

North Stafford Railway Set 21 £8

RAILWAYS

OFFICIALS
Note. Many of the official issues were also overprinted on the reverse for correspondence use; these command a premium over the normal issue (up to 50%). The correspondence cards listed below were only used for that purpose.

Barry
Dock Scene £35
Views Coloured £8

Belfast and County Down
Slieve Donard Hotel (Jotter) £6
Black/White Hotels £8

Bideford, Westward Ho and
  Appledore £15

Caledonian
Vignette Card, pictures both sides £15–£20
Reliable Series Steamers . . . . . £6+
Views – undivided back . . . . . £15–£20
Views coloured £8
Engines/Rolling Stock, coloured . £4–£8
Black/White Glosso Views . . . . £6+
Sepia Glosso Engines £4
Tartan Border Views . . . . . . £6–£8
Posters . . . . £40–£60
Hotels £4
Hotel Posters £15

CR and L & NW (Royal Mail Route &
  West Coast Joint Stock) . . . . £8+

Callander & Oban . . . . £5+

Cambrian
Vignette £25
Views £6
  Correspondence £8
Maps . . . . £20–£25

Campbeltown & Macrihanish . . . £45

Central London
Celesque Series £6
Novelties . . . . £25–£60
Picture & Route Map £15
Posters £30

Cheshire Lines Committee £25

Cork Bandon & South Coast
Oilette Views £4

Cork Blackrock & Passage
Paddle Steamer *Audrey* £30

Cheshire Lines – scarce £25

HHH Series real photo for the Furness Railway £8

Previously Barry Railway's 'Gwalia'
Furness Railway Series 20 £8

The Great Central Railway were the main
user of the HHH photo cards £8

Corris
Photographic Views . . . . £4–£6
Printed Views £8
District Railway
Court Cards £35
Dublin & South Eastern £20
Dublin, Wicklow & Wexford
View, undivided back £25
Peacock Series Correspondence . . £20
Dumbarton & Balloch Joint Line Committee
Views, B/W . . . . £10–£15
Views, Coloured £15
East Coast Route
Vignette . . . . £15–£20
Rolling Stock and Views . . . . £5–£10
Festiniog
Poster £75
Freshwater Yarmouth & Newport
Vignette £30
Furness
McCorquodale Vignette . . . . £15–£20
Views £2.50

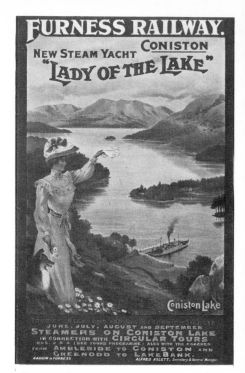

Furness Railway Set 21 – six cards like this for 3d!
£75

Tucks Views £2
Lake Steamers . . . . £4+
G. Romney Paintings £8
Hotels £3
Engines and Rolling Stock £5
Barrow & Fleetwood Steamers . . . £8
Exhibitions £10
Posters £75
Photographic Views £6
Glasgow & South Western
Vignette Views . . . . £20–£25
Oilettes . . . . £4+
Steamers, McCorquodale £1.50
Other £4
Posters £45
Hotels £5
Hotels multi-view . . . . £5–£15
Great Central
Vignette Views . . . . £25+
Immingham Docks £2
Ships (Turner, G. E. & Co) . . . . £10+
Tuck £25

Great Northern Railway advertising holiday
travel in 1905 £65

Undivided back, although not used until 1906 £25

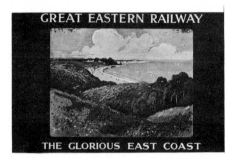

One for the Jotter collectors £40

Not a bad Tram but worth more as
a railway card £12+

Most GWR correspondence cards were
less attractive than this series £12

Great Central (continued)

Views Faulkner	£6
Photographic	£6+
Poster	£60
Shipping Printed	£8
Photographic	£10
Steam Ship Department	£25

Great Eastern

Tuck Vignette	£30
Views B/W	£2+
Coloured (Oilettes)	£2
Hotels	£3.50
Posters	£10–£50
Correspondence Cards	£8–£15
Oilette type (on front)	£15+
Jarrold	£8
Ships	£4–£6
Cathedrals Faulkner with crest	£20–£25
Cathedrals Faulkner Series 119	£10
Greetings from Harwick vignettes	£5+

Great Northern

Vignette Views	£25+
Hotels	£5–£15
Photochrom views engines	£1
Correspondence	£5
Locomotive Publishing Co	£4+
Posters Panoramic Views	£15
Others	£50+

Great Northern Ireland

Views Correspondence	£10
Hotels multi-view	£15
Milroy Bay Bus	£25

Great Northern & City

Views	£10
Posters B/W	£40

Great Northern Piccadilly & Brompton

Views	£4–£6
Map	£20

Great North of Scotland

Views, Porter, Aberdeen	£8
Palace Hotel Series	£10+
Cruden Bay Golf Tournament	£15
Hotel multi-view	£15

Great Southern & Western Ireland

Tuck Oilette Views	£4
Great Southern Hotel	£15
Hotels multi-view	£25+
Views Lawrence	£10+
Jotter	£5
Joint with M.G.W. (Wembley 1924)	£15

Great Western

Views Vignette	£25+
Sepia	£4+
Coloured	£4–£6
Posters, Series 3	£75
Others	£20–£40
Engines	£2+
Hotels Vignettes	£10
Other	£4+
Correspondence	£10
Shipping	£8

Hampstead Tube

Multi-Views, Map on back	£10
Last Link coloured views	£6

Highland

Views (straight line inscription)	£10
(circular crest)	£8
Coloured	£8
Photographic	£10
Hotels	£8–£12

Hull & Barnsley

Views and Dock Scenes	£10–£15

A court card for the London and South Western Railway £40

Invergary & Fort Augustus

Views (Highland Railway Series)	£15–£20

Isle of Wight

Vignette	£25+

Isle of Wight Central

Vignette	£25
View	£30

Joint South Western & Brighton

Vignette	£25

Kent & East Sussex

Views	£8+
Engine	£6

Lancashire & Yorkshire

Vignettes	£20–£25
Views	£1.50+
Overprinted French	£4
Engines	£2+
Overprinted French	£5
Ships	£5+
Overprinted French	£7+
Correspondence	£25

A London and North Western Railway steam railmotor on the Dyserth branch in North Wales £5

Hampstead Tube Series 1,
with a map of the system on the back £10

Golf was popular with many companies – this card
is one of several for the Highland Railway £8+

Memories of fish trains, and the smell that
went with them £25

June 1898 – does anyone know of any earlier
use of a railway card? £40

London, Brighton & South Coast

Vignette	£20–£25
Views Waterlow	£2–£4
Bridges	£3
Correspondence	£12
Posters	£60

London & North Western

St. Louis Exposition undivided back

Tucks B/W	£6–£8
Tucks coloured	£8

Tucks

Engines, Views, Ships, etc. . . .	£1–£2+
Hotels	£2–£4

McCorquodale

Buses, Lorries, etc.	£8–£12
Engines, Views, Ships	£1–£2+
Posters	£30–£60
Hotels	£1–£2

London & South Western

Vignette Black/white	£25
Coloured	£30+
Ships B/W	£3
Coloured Early	£15
Posters	£50
Correspondence, view with crest . .	£25
Orphanage	£4

London, Chatham & Dover

Vignette B/W	£25
Coloured	£30+

Londonderry Lough Swilly

Map	£50

Lynton & Barnstaple

Station and Views (Peacocks) . . .	£6–£8

Maryport & Carlisle

Map	£50

Metropolitan

Views Sepia (Numbered)	£5
Black/white	£10
Maps	£20

Metropolitan District

Photographic	£6

Midland

Vignette B/W	£20
Coloured, Andrew Reid	£25
Maps	£15–£20
Carriages	£10
Ships	£8
Views	£1.50–£4
Engine	£2
Posters	£15–£50

Midland (continued)

Hotels Vignette Col . . . . £5–£7
    Vignette B/W £20
    Others £3

Midland (Northern Counties Committee)

Views (Correspondence) £25
Trains £5

Midland & Great Northern

Correspondence £10

Midland Great Western

Hotels . . . . £4–£6

Newport Godshill & St Lawrence

Vignette . . . . £25+

North British

Views and Ship's Crest on front . . . £10
    Black/white and coloured £8
    Caledonia (129) North British
      Rly Series £6
Scottish Exhibition Poster O/P . . . £25
Ships coloured £8

Railway stands were to be found at
most of the exhibitions £12

North Eastern

Views Photo Panoramic £8
    Maps below picture £20
Posters . . . . £40–£60
Hull Riverside Quay £3
Ships £8
Hotels . . . . £2–£5
Brussels Exhibition £10

North Staffordshire

McCorquodale and W & K views . . . £4+
White border views, W & K and W & TG £6
Golf and Glossy Anon. Views . . . . £6+
Correspondence . . . . £8+

Portpatrick & Wigtownshire Joint

Views . . . . £25–£35
Ships . . . . £20+

South Eastern Chatham (& Dover)

Vignettes Blue Frame etc. £25
    Sepia . . . . £10–£15
McCorquodale Views, etc. £1.50
Correspondence £15
Maps £20
Posters £60
Hotels . . . . £3–£5

Stratford on Avon & Midland Junction

Posters £100

Underground

Posters multi-view £40
    Others . . . . £25–£40
    W.H.S. £10

Vale of Rheidol

Views £8

Weston, Clevedon & Portishead

Views Photographic £25

West Clare

Views . . . . £10+

1908 – will the next Midland electrification be
opened in time for the seventy-fifth anniversary? £15

Metropolitan Railway £5

West Highland
Views £10
Wick & Lybster
Views (Highland R. Series) £10
Wirral
Map £50
LMS, LNER, SR
Trains, Ships . . . . £2–£4
Hotels . . . . £2–£4
Views £3
Posters . . . . £30–£40
Road Vehicles £20
Camping Coaches £6

Detailed listings of the Official Issues are now available in a number of publications. All companies are listed in a series of 20 booklets by Alsop/Hilton/Wright. Two books by J. Silvester cover LNWR and GWR, GCR, Cambrian, etc. Please refer to bibliography.

One of 20 published by the North Eastern Railway in 1908 £60

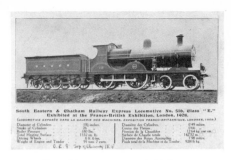

Everything you ever wanted to know on this SECR exhibition card £6

TRAINS & ENGINES
This section has been simplified as prices of this type of card tend to fall within the ranges quoted despite the publisher or artist.
Printed, B/W 75
   Coloured . . . . £1+
   Tuck Oilette . . . . £2+
Photographic P/C back 75
Loco Publishing Co.
   Printed Vignette Coloured . . . £25+
   B/W . . . . £15–£25
   Full size Coloured . . . . . £1.50+
   B/W . . . . £1+
   Photographic . . . . . . 50–£1.50

See supplement to 1982 Pictons for listings of the main coloured series.

STATIONS *see Topographical*
Narrow Gauge . . . . £4–£10
Miniature . . . . £1.50+
Foreign . . . . . value about ½–¾ British

Miscellaneous
Accidents & Disasters . . . . . £4–£6
Bridges & Viaducts, Tunnels . . . 75+
Level Crossings . . . . £2+
Permanent Way . . . . 75+
Motor Buses – close-up . . . £15–£40
Mountain Railways . . . . . 50–£2
Lifts (cliff), etc. . . . . 50+
Modern coloured cards 25–50

French Poster Cards
UB Chromo-Litho £20
Artist signed . . . . . . £4–£15
Orleans post–1920 . . . . £4

H.R.H. THE PRINCE OF WALES.
Inspecting the first process of FRAME DYEING at JOHNSONS' DYE WORKS, Bootle, July 5th, 1921.

Royal Visits, The Prince of Wales at Johnson's Dye Works 1921 £4

THE ROYAL VISIT TO LIVERPOOL. JULY 1927. T.R. 14.

Royal Visits, Geo V and Queen Mary riding through Liverpool 1927 £3

ROYALTY

BRITISH ROYALTY
QUEEN VICTORIA
Diamond Jubilee 1897 unused	. . . £75
Used in 1897	. . . . . . £100–£150
Portraits	. . . . £6–£10
Mourning Cards 1901	. . . . . £15–£20

EDWARD VII
Coronation Souvenir 1902	. . . . . £8
Coronation Procession 1902	. . . £1.50
Royal Tour (Tuck)	
Prince & Princess of Wales	. . . . £8
Others	. . . . £6
Set postally used at all stops	. . £200
Mourning Cards 1910	. . . . £3
Funeral Procession 1910	. . . . . . £1
Visits, G.B.	. . . . £3+
Foreign	. . . . £1.50

GEORGE V
Coronation Souvenir 1911	. . . . . £3
Coronation Procession 1911	. . . . £1
Investiture of Prince of Wales	. . . . £3
Silver Jubilee Souvenir 1935	. . . £2.50

A Royal Fisherman £2

Silver Jubilee Procession 1935	. . . 60
Mourning Cards 1936	. . . . . . £2.50
Processions	 75
Visits, G.B.	. . . . £2.50–£4
Foreign	. . . . £2+

EDWARD VIII
Visits, Local 1936	. . . . £4–£6
Visits Foreign	. . . . £4
Coronation Souvenir	. . . . £3
Portraits	. . . . £1.50–£2.50

GEORGE VI
Coronation 1937	. . . . £2.50
Procession	 60
Victory Celebrations 1945	 75
Mourning Cards 1952	. . . . £3
Visits Local	. . . . £3+
Foreign	. . . . £1.50

ELIZABETH II
Coronation 1953	. . . . 75–£2
Procession	 50
Visits, Local 1953	. . . . £1.50
Investiture of Prince of Wales	. . . £1.50
Portraits Photographic black/white	£1–£2

French souvenir card for George V Coronation visit
£3

Coloured	£1.50
Foreign Visits	£1.50+
Silver Jubilee Souvenir	50
Queen Mother's 80th Birthday	30
Prince Charles and	
Lady Diana Spencer Engagement .	25
Prince & Princess of Wales	20+

MISCELLANEOUS

Royal Weddings	£1.50–£2.50
Gatherings	75–£1.50

FOREIGN ROYALTY
Portraits

Russian	£6
East European	£4
Others	£1.50–£3.50
Embossed Souvenir Cards . . .	£8–£15

Above right: Royal Weddings have
always produced attractive cards £3

Below left: German Tuck Oilette for
Jubilee 1913 £5

Below right: Artist C. Monestier's portrait
of Italian King Victor Emanuel III £3

SHIPPING

NAVAL
Battleships/Cruisers
Tuck 'Empire' Series, Vign. £12
   Oilette Series £2
G.B. Types pre-1939
   Art type £1.25
   Photo type £1.50
Foreign types pre-1939
   Art type . . . . 50–£1
   Photo type . . . . 50–£1
Others (1939 onwards) . . . . 30+
Launchings £3

Life in the Navy
Cork, F. (Invicta Series) 40
Ettlinger, Max (Life in our Navy) . . . 40
Gale & Polden 50
G.D. & D. London (Star Series) . . . 30
Kelkel Series 40
Knight Series 40
National Series 50
Photochrom Co. (Britain Prepared
   Series) 50
Tuck, R. & Sons (Oilette Series) . . £1.50
Other photographic types . . . . 30+

Other Naval
Submarines pre-1939 . . . . £2
Special Interest (Fleet Reviews/
   Displays, etc.) . . . . 75–£1.50
Naval Vessels (Torpedo Boats, etc.) . 75
Sailor's photographs, etc. 30

Lord Nelson Cards
Trafalgar Day Souvenir 1905 . . . . £3
Life of Nelson/Oilette Series
   (Tuck, R. & Sons) £1
Life of Nelson/Nelson Series
   (Gale & Polden) 50
Life of Nelson (Woolstone Bros.) . . 50
Life of Nelson (Other issues) 40
H.M.S. Victory (Gale & Polden) . . . 30
H.M.S. Victory (Other issues) 20

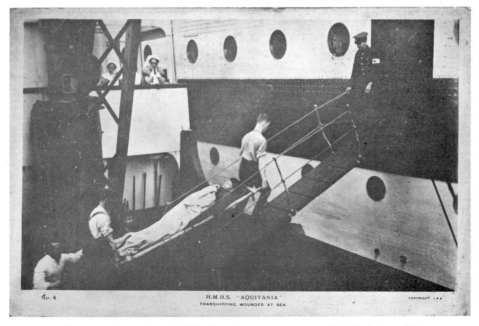

The 'Aquitania' as a Hospital Ship. These have become very popular in the last year £4

MERCHANT SHIPPING

N.B. Most coloured and some B/W cards were issued by the Shipping Companies and are, therefore, 'Official Company Publicity' types. *For Woven Silk Ships see Silks*

Advertising Postcards

Poster type	
(issued by Shipping Lines)	£15–£25
Company Publicity type (vign.)	£15
Other early issues	£8–£12
Later Issues	£2–£5

Merchant Ships

Lusitania	£3
(in memoriam cards)	£4
Titanic (photo type)	
Actual	£6–£10
'Olympic'	£4
In memoriam cards	£8–£10
Art type	£4
Oilette Series (Tuck, R. & Sons)	£6
Other Liners (pre-1939) Coloured	£2.50–£4
Black/white	£2
Photo	£1.50–£2
Other Liners (1939 onwards)	£1.50
Oilette Series (Tuck, R. & Sons)	£4
Launchings	£3–£5
Interior photographs	£1+
Japanese Official	£4
Japanese Official Embossed	£6+
Cargo Boats/Tugs, etc.	£1.50–£2.50
Coastal Vessels	£2.50+
Modern Cards/Reproductions	25

Miscellaneous

Accidents/Wrecks	
G.B. Photo	£4–£10
Printed	£4–£6
Foreign	£1–£3
Coastguards/Stations	£1
Convict Hulks	£2
Docks/Harbours	£1–£4
Ferries River	75+
Cross Channel	£1.50+

Early chromolithograph official Allan Royal Mail Line card printed by Wm Strain & Sons, Belfast £12

Cunard Line official card £2.50

Broadstairs harbour with sailing barge £2.50

A trip round the wreck £3

Miscellaneous (continued)

Fishing Industry	£1.50+
(Boats/Fishermen, etc.) Col.	£1–£2.50
Photo	£3–£8
Historic Vessels	
(Wooden Walls, etc.)	50–£1
Houseboats (identified)	£1.50
Lifeboats	
Photo	£6–£8
Printed	£4–£6
Crews	£4–£6
Parades	£6–£10
'Inland Launchings'	£6–£8
Lighthouses	75–£1.50
Lightships	£2.50
Paddle Steamers, G.B.	£3–£5
Foreign	75–£3
Pleasure Boats (identified)	£1+
Royal Yacht (Victoria and Albert)	£1.50–£2
Sailing Barges photo	£4–£6+
Printed	£2–£4
Sailing Ships photo	
(Square Riggers, etc.)	£4

Union-Castle Line Poster showing RMMS 'Carnarvon Castle' £20

Shipyards	£2–£4
Special Interest	
(Hull Trawler Outrage)	£2–£3
Yachts (River types)	75
(Sea types)	75

ARTISTS

Cumming, Neville	£1.50–£2.50
Dunn, James S.	£2
Fry, John H.	£2.50
Lacy, Chas. J. de	£2.50
Meade-Gibbs	£1.25
Rosenvinge, Odin	£3
Shoesmith, Kenneth . . .	£2.50–£3.50
Stower, Willi	
Early	£8–£10
Later	£3

Cox'n Blogg, RNLI medal winner £5.50

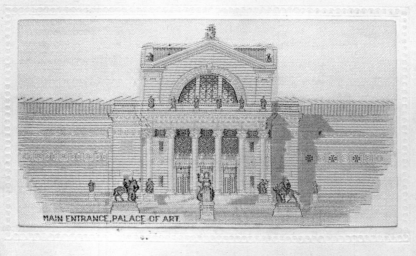

Woven silk for the Louisiana Purchase Exposition 1904. Very rare £60

A Nova card for pier collectors and our local card £20

SILKS

This is a vast and complex subject and because of the rarity of some silk postcard designs, it is impossible to quote accurate prices. We have, therefore, used the plus sign (+) to indicate a range of prices with an undefined upper limit. Those needing further information, please see Bibliography.

WOVEN SILKS

W.H. Grant & Co
Exhibitions . . . . £25–£80
Portraits . . . . £35–£60
Ships . . . . £25–£60
Hands Across the Sea
   (Ships & Greetings) . . . . . £30–£60
Views . . . . £20–£50
Subjects . . . . £30–£75
Greetings (Songs & Hymns) . . £20–£35

Thomas Stevens
Portraits . . . . £40+
Religious Subjects . . . . £35+
Views . . . . £20–£150
Subjects . . . . £30–£135
Ships
   Liners, Steamers &
    Landing Stages . . . . . . £25–£60
   Transports . . . . £40–£65
   Battleships . . . . £80–£150
Hands Across the Sea . . . . . £20–£60

Alpha Series
(Designs produced by Stevens
   for Alpha Publishing Co.)
Greetings . . . . £15–£20
Flag Designs . . . . £40–£50
Stevens Designs . . . . £25–£40

Early German
H.M. Krieger (views & subjects) . £35–£60
Rudolf Knuffman (portraits,
   views & subjects) . . . . . . £40+
Other Early German . . . . . . £30+

French
A. Benoiston (Paris Exposition 1900) . £50
Neyret Frères
1904 Series Art Nouveau, Classical
   and Portraits . . . . . . £35–£125
1906 Series Views, Portraits &
   Art Nouveau . . . . . . £35–£100
1907–1918 Series Classical . . . £15–£50
*(N.B. Some of these designs
are also found in full colour.)*
1915–1917 Series
   B/W Portraits & Patriotics . . . £15–£50
   Coloured . . . . £25–£45
1916–1918 Series Flames
   (Common designs, e.g. Albert, Martyr,
   Ypres, etc.) £12
   Other Designs . . . . £15–£80
1917–1918 Series Greetings . . . £10–£30
Bertrand & Boiron Portraits . . . . £30+
Other Early European . . . . . £25–£40

Japanese
Views & Portraits . . . . £40–£60
   (with Grant-type A/N mounts) . . . £25

United States
St. Louis 1904 Exposition . . . . . £60+

Designs Printed on Fabric
Flames – Edition Gabriel . . . . £8–£12
Edith Cavell (Plain Backs) £1.50
Lord Kitchener £6
FAB Patchwork (W.N. Sharpe)
   Flowers £5
   Heraldic Designs £8
   Views £8
   Royalty £15
FAB Patchwork Pat, 735 (Gaunt,
   Armley) £6
   Stage Stars . . . . £8–£10
Cinema Stars (Plain Backs) 75
Miscellaneous printed £2
Stewart & Woolf Series 497 Glamour . £6

EMBROIDERED

Early (Pre-1910) . . . . £5–£15

WW1
Patriotic (Flags, etc.) £3
Floral & Sentimental £1.50

Regimental Badges
Line Regiments . . . . . . £12–£18+
Corps (ASC, RE, RFA, etc.) £6
Royal Navy/RNVR £10
Named Battleships . . . . £25+
Royal Air Force/RFC £10
Army Camps . . . . £10–£12
Commonwealth Regiments . . . £15+

Personalities
Inset Photos – Single . . . . £8+
– Double . . . . £12+
Name Embroidered £15
Miss Cavell . . . . £20+

Heraldic
British Towns . . . . £12–£15
European Towns/Countries £5
Overseas Towns . . . . . . £15–£20
Countries . . . . £8–£20

Better Designs
Cartoons . . . . £8–£10
Views . . . . £6–£8
Aircraft, guns, etc. . . . . £5–£6
Salvation Army £15
Santas £6

Year Dates
1914–1919 . . . . £5
1920–1923 . . . . £6
1925–1939 . . . . £8
1940 . . . . £4
1945 . . . . £8

Add these amounts to the basic card where applicable
Celluloid Inserts £1
Envelope Type 75
Silk Handkerchief £2.50
Inserts – War Scenes £1.50
Perfumed £1
Artist Signed £1.50

Machine Embroidered
Broderie d'Art (R. Tuck) £3
Birn Brothers (These are embossed coloured cards with silk insets) . £3–£8
Spanish – Early £6
Later 75

A charming 'better design'.
In this condition about £5

SPORT

Angling 75
Archery £1.50
Athletics
  Athletes (known) £2
  Stadiums £3
  Olympic Games . . . . . . £4–£10+
Baseball 50
Billiards/Snooker . . . . £2+
Boxing
  Amateur £1.50
  Professional £2.50
Bullfighting
  Photo 75
  Art Type 30
Cricket
  Players
    Photo £4
    Printed £4
    Signed . . . . £5+

Cricket – Australia 1921 signatures £3

Bisley 1907 £3

Opening of a Football Ground £8

Teams
  Photo £4
  Printed £3.50
  International £3.50
  Grounds . . . . £1.50–£4
  Comics . . . . £1+
  Kinsella £1.50
Cycle Racing, etc. *see under Transport*
Football
  Amateur Teams . . . . £3.50+
  Amateur Grounds . . . . . . £2–£4
  Professional Players £5
  Teams £5
  Memorium Cards . . . . £6+
  Commemorative Cards . . . . . £5–£8
  Modern 50
  Crowd Scenes £1.50
  Comics . . . . £1–£2
  Kinsella £1.50
Rugby
  Players £4
  Teams . . . . £4+

Golf
Players (named)	£4–£6
Courses	£1–£1.50
Comics	£2–£4
Product Advert N.B.R.	£5–£30
Tournaments	£5

Horse Jumping
Show Advertising	£3–£5
Riders	£1

Horse Racing
Courses	£1–£2
Grandstands	£1–£2
Jockeys	£2.50
Horses (Black/white)	£1.50
(Coloured)	£2
'Kromo' Series, B & D	£1.50
Racing Colours, Wildt & Kray . . .	£2
Everetts Sporting Series (H. Bird)	£2.50
Tuck 'Derby Winners'	£3
Famous Racehorse S. 3494	£3
Wrench Series	£1.50
Meissner & Buch Series 1003	
(C. Becker)	£8

Hunting by G. Koch £2.50

Tuck Popular Racing Colours	
(Dink)	£3.50

Artists
Elliott, Harry	£5
Koch, Ludwig	£3.50
Lehmann, Felix	£3
Mason, Finch	£2

Hunting
Art	75–£1.50
Photo (named)	£1.50–£2.50

Rules of Golf – Comic Version £2.50

WILL HE LIFT IT ?

The leading Physical Culture Magazine.
2d. monthly, from all Bookstalls.

Health & Strength Magazine advert with political caricature £5

ARTHUR RUSSELL,
OF THE THOMSON-HOUSTON A.C., RUGBY, WHO WILL REPRESENT
GREAT BRITAIN AND IRELAND IN THE 3,200 METRES STEEPLE-
CHASE CHAMPIONSHIP OF THE WORLD, AT THE OLYMPIC
GAMES OF LONDON, 1908.

Olympics – pre-publicity for 1908 £6

Motor Sport *see under Transport*

Mountaineering	50
Olympics	£4–£10+
Rowing (named)	£1.50
Shooting	
Bisley	£2+
Others	£1.50+
Speedway	
Riders pre-war	£3.50
Post-war	£1
Swimming	
Channel	£1.50
Miscellaneous	50
Table Tennis	
Players	£3.50
Comic	£3

Tennis	
Players	£3
Courts	75+
Kinsella	£2.50
Walking (Racing)	£1+
Winter Sports	
Skiing	50
Skating	50
Tobogganing	50
Wrestling & Body Building . . .	£2.50+

Winkleigh, Devon superb street scene £8

Isle of Wight, Broderick card of Brading £6

TOPOGRAPHICAL

Lower Froyle, Hants, Post Office £8

Hampole Railway Station £8

VILLAGE SCENES	Photo	Printed
Animated Main Streets	£8–£10	£5+
Ordinary Street Scenes	£6+	£3–£5
Post Offices, Close-up	£8+	£6–£8
Post Offices, Middle Distance	£5	£3–£5
Public Houses	£4–£6	£4
Shop Fronts	£8	£4–£6
Local Farms	£3+	£2+
Manor Houses	75	60
Railway Stations, Interiors	£8+	£8
Railway Stations, Exteriors	£6–£8	£6+
Events	£3–£5	£3+
Churches and Chapels	75–£1.50	50–75

TOWNS		
Superb Animated Street Scenes	£10–£15	
Animated Main Streets	£8–£10	£6
Other Street Scenes	£6–£8	£4–£6
Post Offices (Main)	£5+	£4+
Post Offices (Sub)	£6–£8	£6–£8
Public Houses	£4+	£4+
Hotels	£4	£3.50
Shop Fronts	£6–£8	£6+
Parades of Shops	£6	£5+
Railway Stations Interiors	£8+	£8
Railway Stations, Exteriors	£6–£8	£6+
Events	£3–£5	£3–£5
Churches and Chapels	75–£1.50	50–75

MAJOR CITIES/TOWNS including London	Photo	Printed
Main Streets and City Centres (Common views) . . .	30	20
(Unusual views can of course command high prices.)		
Animated Suburban Streets	£8–£10	£4–£6
Side Roads and Streets	£3–£6	£2–£4
Cathedrals	20	20
Church and Chapels, Suburban	75–£1	50–75
Events	£4–£6	£3–£5
Post Offices		
Suburban	£6–£8	£6+
Main Exteriors	75	75
Railway Stations		
Central Interior	£1.50–£3	£1–£3
Exterior	75–£1.50	50–£1
Suburban Interior	£8+	£8
Exterior	£6–£8	£6+
Shop Fronts	£6–£8	£6+
Hotels	50–£3	50–£3

Horse sale for WWI at Southwell by H. Barrett £8

Floods at Salisury £7

MISCELLANEOUS

	Photo	Printed
Abbeys	20	20
Aerial Views	£1.50	£1.50
Bridges	£1	75
Castles	50	50
Cinemas/Bioscopes see under Entertainment		
Comic (Town names)		£1.50
Docks/Harbours	£2–£4	£1–£3
Heraldic see under Heraldic		
H.T.L. see under Novelty		

Better view of landslip at Lowestoft £5

L.&N.W.R. bus at Brownhills £16

	Photo	Printed
Hotels – early Adverts		£3–£5
Hospitals	£1–£3	£1–£3
Markets, Places	£4–£8	£2–£4
Markets, Street	£5–£8+	£4+
Monuments	30–50	30–50
Pull Outs (Town names)		£1.50+
Royal Visits	£4–£6	£4+
Schools	£1–£1.50	£1–£1.50

Artists' Views (*for name of Artist see under Artist section*). These cards are becoming more popular and prices are gradually moving.

DISASTERS

	Photo	Printed
Coast Erosion	£2+	£1+
Earthquakes	£1.50	75
Explosions	£6–£8	£6
Fires	£6–£8	£6
Floods	£4–£6	£3–£6
Lightning Damage	£4+	£3+
Memoriam Disaster Cards	£8+	£8+
Gothards	£15–£25	
Snow Damage	£3+	£2+
Storm Damage	£2.50+	£1.50
Subsidence	£6	£4–£6
Volcanoes	60	30
Wrecked Buildings	£4–£6	£3–£5
Wrecked Piers	£6–£8	£2–£4

For other disaster postcards see under subject headings, e.g. Industry.

MAPS

Bacon Excelsior Series £4
Comic Maps 40
Cyclists' Touring Club (C.T.C.) . . . £4
Early Maps £4
Embossed type £3.50
Mountain Tracks (mainly Swiss) . . . 75
Walkers Geographical Series £4

SEASIDE

General Views 25–50
Bathing Huts . . . . 50–£1
Bathing Huts (close-up) . . . . . £1–£2
Piers . . . . 50–£1+
Donkeys & Children 40
Pierrots . . . . £1.50+
Punch & Judy Shows . . . . £5+
Sandcastles (photo type) £1
Superb Photo Beach Scenes . . £1.50+

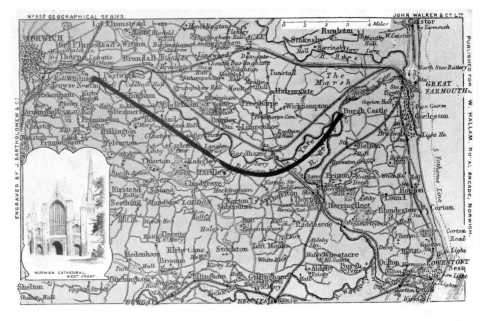

Bartholomew's map card showing proposed route for **Norwich and Yarmouth Ship Canal**. Despite holes £6

The Village Pump at Winkleigh, Devon £8

North Somercotes Windmill by
A. Loughton of Southwell £8

	Photo	Printed
WATERMILLS		
Close-up	£3–£6	£2–£4
Middle Distance	£2–£4	£1–£2
Art Type		50+
WINDMILLS		
Close-up	£8–£10	£5–£8
Middle Distance	£4–£6	£3–£5
Art Type		75+
Foreign		£1+
Disasters	£15	

For **Foreign Views** see **Overseas** section. For **Transport** see under.

For **List of Publishers** see 1982 Edition.

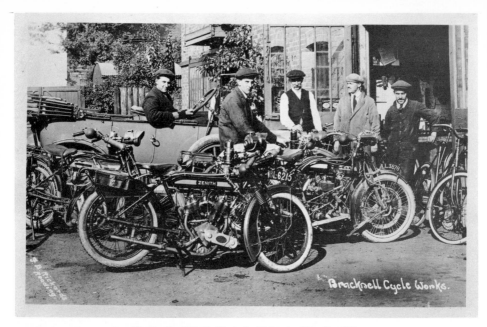

The Bracknell Cycle Works by Richards of Reading £15

Ipswich St John Ambulance Brigade Lifeboat Collection by H. R. Tunn £12

TRANSPORT

AVIATION
Aircraft
Aviation Meetings,
   Poster Advert B/W £20
   Coloured £30
   At Named Towns £15
Brooklands Aviation £8
Daily Mail Tour 1912 . . . . £6+
   Aircraft at named localities . . £12–£15
Flying at Hendon £6
Pre-1918
   Private £8
   Accidents . . . . £8–£12
   Military . . . . £4+
Imperial Airways
   Officials . . . . £5+
   Pilots . . . . £8+
Overseas Nat. Airlines . . . . . . £2–£5
Art Types
   Tucks, etc. . . . . £4–£6
   Later, Salmon, etc. £3
Pre-1940 . . . . £2–£4
W.W.2 50
Modern Airlines £1.50
Rockets pre-1939 . . . . £1.50
   W.W.2 50
   1950 to date . . . . 30+

Airships
Pre-1918 Military £8
Zeppelins W.W.1
   Combat (Printed) £2
   Shot down . . . . £4–£8
   Civil photo (see note) £8
British R101, etc. £8

Miscellaneous
Airfields . . . . £3–£5
   Croydon . . . . £5+
Gliding £1.50
Pilots
   Early Aviators . . . . £6–£8
   Military (Aces) £6
   W.W.2 . . . . £3

Used and Flown cards are worth considerably more in many cases. Other overseas – these are very difficult to catalogue as it depends on the home market and philatelic interest.

Grahame White leaving Poleworth £12

Continental card for Imperial Airways Helena – unusual £6

Tuck's 'In the Air' Series 111 No 3201 £4

R34 Beagles postcard 168W £8

Goods inside! Passengers on top! Superb Bournemouth bus by R.B. Brown £75

AMBULANCES
Horse (photo) . . . . £15+
Motor (photo) . . . . £4–£6
Motor (print) £3
   identified . . . . £4+

BICYCLES
Close-up (photo) £3
Advert. Poster . . . . £25+
Cycling
   Military (photo) £1.50
   Social (photo) . . . . £2+
   Racing (photo) . . . . £3+

BUSES
Horse, close-up (photo) . . . . £25–£35
Print . . . . £10–£20
Horse, middle-distance (photo) . £10–£15
   Print . . . . £8+
Motor, close-up (photo) . . . . £25–£50
   Print . . . . £12–£20
Poorly printed, sometimes coloured, London buses are only worth . . . £5–£10
Middle distance (photo) . . . . £12–£15
   Print . . . . £8–£10
Street Scenes Local
   Photo . . . . £8–£10
   Print . . . . £4–£6

CANALS
Aqueducts £4
Boats & Barges (close-up) . . . £10–£20
   (general views) . . . . £4–£6
   (Family groups) . . . . . . £10–£15
Canal construction/workers . . . £10+
Disasters . . . . £10–£20
Feeders £5
Foreign canals £2.50
Inland Waterways Officials . . . . . 50+
   (modern) 25
Locks and Bridges . . . . £3+
Military Canals £1.50
Narrow Canals . . . . £2–£5
Ship Canals . . . . £1–£3
Tunnels . . . . £3–£5
N.B. Because of scarcity, there is little difference between photographic or printed cards, although exceptional photographs will always command a large premium, the sum of £70 being obtained this year for one card.

Worcester's new motor fire engine! £8

	Photo	Printed
CHARABANCS		
Close-up	£2.50+	
Middle distance	£1	
FIRE ENGINES AND CREW (identified)		
Horse drawn	£15–£20	£10–£15
Motor driven	£10–£15	£8–£12
Firemen	£6	£4–£6
LORRIES (identified)		
Steam (close-up)	£15–£25	
Motor (close-up)	£6–£8	
Advertising cards		£6
MOTOR CARS (Early)		
Close-up	£4	
Advertising		£5–£10
Advertising Poster		£15–£35
MOTOR CYCLES (Early)		
Close-up	£4	
With sidecar	£5+	
Advertising	£4	£6+
RACING CARS		
Brooklands	£8+	£6+
Peking–Paris		£10
Others	£1.50–£4	£1.50–£4
RACING – MOTOR CYCLES		
Close-up	£4	£4
Personalities		£2–£3

	Photo	Printed
TRACTION ENGINES		
Close-up	£20	
Middle distance	£6–£8	£4–£6
Road Scenes	£4–£6	£4–£6
Accidents	£15–£25	£8–£10
TRAMS		
Horse Drawn		
Close-up	£25–£35	£15+
Middle distance	£15	£8+
In Memoriam		£10–£15
Steam		
Close-up	£15–£25	£8–£15
Middle distance	£8+	£6+
Street Scenes	£4–£6	£4–£6
In Memoriam		£10+

Foden No 7460 produced 1917. Taken in 1926 whilst used by Oxford C.C., Geo Hickman driving £20

Electric		
Track Laying	£8–£12	£8+
B.O.T. Trial Runs	£15–£25	£10–£15
Opening Ceremonies	£15–£25	£15+
Commemorative cards	£15–£25	£15+
Close-up	£15–£25	£10–£15
Middle distance	£8–£12	£6–£10
Street Scenes	£6–£8	£4–£6

First electric car at Horsforth. Not rare but gorgeous! £22

Miscellaneous

Accidents	£15–£25	£8–£15
Comic		£1.50+
Decorative/Illuminated	£6–£10	£6+
Terminii (with trams)	£8–£15	£8–£12
Sheds/Depots	£12–£20	£8–£12
Works Vehicles	£15–£25	
In Memoriam	£10–£15	£10+

FOREIGN it is impossible to price this vast field which depends on the popularity of the home market, but a *very general* guide would be about two-thirds of the prices above.

TROLLEY Buses

Close-up (early)	£8–£12	
Street Scenes	£4+	£3+

Note: These are very rare but little collected.

MODERN TRANSPORT

Pamlin Prints	15
Reproductions	25+

See also **Comic** section for Transport types.

Early 'Art' Postcard Series 963. £10

Another 'Oilette' Series 6231. 'General Booth' £3

A privately produced Oilfacsim card for the
County Fire Office. Cheap at £2.50

'Oilette' Series 6441.
Tom Browne's 'Seaside Humour' £6

TUCK, R. & SON

The firm of Tucks have produced more post-cards than any other company in the post-card world. It would require a catalogue larger than this to cover all their issues, so only some of the more collected ones are listed – other Tuck cards will be found listed under subject headings, or under Artists where appropriate.

It may be of interest to collectors to know that the firm's complete records of their issues were destroyed in the Second World War.

Animal Life	
Early Vignettes	£6–£8
Later issues	£1.50
Animal Studies	50
Antique Deckle-Edged Collotype	30
Aquarette	40
Art, Early Vignettes	£6–£8
Middle period	£1
Later issues	30
Art Collotype	20

Continental Series 4033

Art Glosso Greeting	30
Bathing Girls	£2–£4
Birthday, Middle period	£1.50
Later issues	30
British Navy, Early Vignettes	£12
British Sports	£1
Broderie d'Art	£3
Calendar	£1.50
Carbonette	20
Celebrities of the Stage	35
Charmette	20
Christmas, Early Vignettes	£6
Middle period	£1
Later issues	30
Chromette	20
Collo-Photo	30
Collotype	20
Coloured Crayon	30+
Connoisseur, Middle period	£1.50
Later issues	40
Continental	30+
Continental Art	50+

Connoisseur Series 2557 £3

Country Life	75–£1.50
County	75–£1.50
Crayon	20
Dog Studies	75–£1.50
Double Photo Greeting	20
Duo Gem	20
Early Tuck No. Cards 1–10	£125 set
Easter, Early Vignettes	£6
Middle period	£1.50
Later issues	50
Educational	£6
Elite	£1.50
Emerald Rough Sea	20
Emerald Sea	20
Empire, Early Vignettes	£10–£15
Fair Flowers	75
Floral Gems	75
Flower	20
Framed Aquagraph	30
Charmette	20
Gem Glosso	20
Gem Tartan	75+
Marble	20

Oilette 'The Gentle Art of Making Love' Series 9492

Gem Glosso	20
Gem Oilette	50
Glosso	20
Golden Amber Glosso	20
Gold Framed Gravure	20
Greeting, Middle period	£1+
Later issues	30
Hand Coloured Photogravure	20
Heraldic, Early Vignettes	£8
Heraldic, View	£1
Holly	£1
Impressionist	£2–£3
Independence Day	£4
Kings & Queens of England	£8
Landseer, Early Vignettes	£4
Little Hollander	£1.50
London	£1
Marine, Early Vignettes	£8–£12
Monogram	£5
New Year, Middle period	£1+
Later issues	50
North Wales	20
Oilette	30+

LONDON.
IN THE STRAND.

Aquarette Series 6166

Oilette Connoisseur	50
Oilette de Luxe	50
Olde Print	50
Photochrome	30
Photographic Pictures	50
Photogravure	20
Plate Marked	60
Quaint Corners	50
Rapholette	20
Rapholette Glosso	20
Raphotype	10
Realistic Roses	20
Real Japanese	£2
Real Photograph	20
Rembrandtesque	30
Remembrance	£1+
Rough Sea	20+
Rural England	60
Rural Life	£1
Sapphire Rough Sea	20
Scottish Rough Sea	20
Sepia	20
Silverette	40

Oilette 'Wide Wide World' Series 3495 £2.50

Sporting	£2
Sweet Sixteen	£1.50
Thanksgiving	£3
Time of Flowers	60
Town and City	£1.50
Turneresque	£1.50
United Kingdom	£1.25
Valentine Posies	£1.50
View, Early Vignettes	£6–£15
Later issues	50+
Water Colour	20
Wide Wide World	50–£3+
Write Ahead, Early Vignettes	£4.50
Write Away, Early Vignettes	£4
Later issues	£2
Young Folks	50
Proof Editions, 1000 copies	£8+
Proof Editions in sets with cover (complete as issued)	£50–£75

View Postcard No 803, at least £6

Not-so-Poker-faces! What a playing card! £7.50

Enough to make any postcard collector cry – fire at Gale & Polden's, Aldershot 1918.

MISCELLANEOUS

Archaeology	50+
Bray signed postcards	£3.50
Casinos	£2.50
Caves	75–£1.50
Cameras	£2–£5
Clocks – Church and Town Hall	25
Floral	25
Coaching	
Maggs Series	75
Coaches, Art	£1.50+
Photo	£3–£10+
Eyes	30
Executions	£3+
Exploration	
Buchanan;Sahara	£5
Others	£2+
Exploration, Polar	
Belgian Antarctic Expedition	£12
Nansen	£10
Peary	£3–£5
Scott 1905	£6+
Scott 1912	£6+
Scottish National Expedition	£15
Shackleton	£4–£8
Others	£4–£10
Flowers	25

Round the World for a Wager.
A particularly good one £5

Flowers/Fruit – still life	50
Fruit	25
Friendly Societies	£1.50+
Gambling (Playing Cards)	£3–£5
Gramophones	£2–£5
Insects, etc.	25
Jewellery	20
Masonic	£3–£6
Models	30
Model Making	60
Opium smoking	£1.50+
Photography	£1.50+
Pottery	20
Pornography	£6–£15
Smoking (comic type)	£1–£1.50
Round the World Journeys	£3–£5
Telephones	50–£2
Trees	50
Trophies, etc.	40
Torture	£2–£5
Waterfalls (British)	30+
(Foreign)	50–£1.50
Wireless	
Pictures of	£2
Comics	£1.50–£2.50

Gramophones – like this about £2

THE EVOLUTION OF THE POSTCARD (1869–1918)

1st Oct. 1869	First postcard issued (World's first)
1st Oct. 1870	G.B. issued her first postcard.
1st April 1872	G.B. privately printed postcards allowed.
9th Oct. 1874	First meeting of the Universal Postal Union.
1st July 1875	G.B. issued her first 1$\frac{1}{4}$d postcard for foreign use.
1st April 1879	G.B. issued two new foreign postcards.
1st May 1882	First exhibition postcard issued (Nuremberg).
1st Oct. 1882	G.B. first reply postcard issued.
1st Sept. 1894	Privately printed cards for use with adhesive stamps allowed in G.B.
1894	First British picture postcard issued by Messrs Geo. Stewart.
21st Jan. 1895	First official court size card issued in G.B.
16th June 1897	Writing on address side of a postcard no longer forbidden by G.P.O.
1st Nov. 1899	U.P.U. size postcards allowed into G.B.
July 1900	Picture postcard magazine published.
Jan. 1902	Divided back postcards allowed in G.B.
21st June 1904	Metal postcards not allowed in the post unless under cover.
5th Sept. 1905	Postcards posted in transparent envelopes no longer allowed in G.B.
June 1906	U.P.U. accepted the divided back postcard.
April 1907	Min. size of postcard raised to 4″ by 2$\frac{3}{4}$″ from 3$\frac{1}{4}$″ by 2$\frac{1}{4}$″.
4th June 1907	Tinsel type postcards could only be sent under cover.
9th Sept. 1911	First U.K. official aerial postcard.
4th Aug. 1914	First World War started.
14th Sept. 1915	Postcards to neutral countries subject to censorship.
2nd May 1916	Names, etc. of H.M. Ships not allowed on postcards.
3rd June 1918	Postcard postage raised to 1d.
11th Nov. 1918	1st World War ended.
Dec. 1918	Censorship of postcards ended.

THE STAMP

Postcards have always been allowed to pass through the post at the minimum postage rate. As a result only low denomination stamps were used which are of little value today, even in quantity. Inland Postage rates on postcards for our period were as follows:

> 1 October 1870 – 3 June 1918 – ½d
> 3 June 1918 – 13 June 1921 – 1d
> 13 June 1921 – 24 May 1922 – 1½d
> 24 May 1922 – 1 May 1940 – 1d

Allowing for foreign rates, twenty-two issues were commonly used on postcards during this period. Prices for regular usage, first day postmarks (all of which are scarce) and some of the varieties are given below used on postcards.

Queen Victoria (died 1901)
1d Lilac (16 dots in each corner) issued 12 December 1881
Regular Usage (overseas) £3
Broken frame varieties £60
½d Vermilion. Issued 1 January 1887
Regular Usage, Inland £1.50
As above but pair (overseas) £3
½d Blue-green
First Day Card, 17 April 1900 . . . . £500
Regular Usage, Inland £1
As above but pair (overseas) £3

King Edward VII (1901–10)
½d Blue-green
First Day Card, 1 January 1902 . . . . £75
Regular Usage, Inland 10p
As above but pair (overseas) 25p
Broken frame varieties £1
1d Red
First Day Card, 1 January 1902 . . . . £75
Regular Usage (overseas) 25p
Broken frame varieties £1
½d Yellow-green
First Day Card, 26 November 1904 . . . . £50
Regular Usage, Inland 5p
As above but pair (overseas) 15p
Minor frame breaks 50p
With St Andrew's Cross attached £150

King George V (1910–1936)

½d Green (Three-quarter profile by Downey, hair dark)

First Day Card, 22 June 1911 . . . . £60

Regular Usage, Inland 35p

As above but pair (overseas) 75p

1d Red (Three-quarter profile by Downey, lion unshaded)

First Day Card, 22 June 1911 . . . . £75

Regular Usage (overseas) 60p

No cross on crown £40

½d Green (Three-quarter profile by Downey, hair light)

First Day Card, 1 January 1912 . . . . £75

Regular Usage, Inland 20p

As above but pair (overseas) 50p

No cross on crown £10

No cross on crown and broken frame £25

1d Red (Three-quarter profile by Downey, lion shaded)

First Day Card, 1 January 1912 . . . . £100

Regular usage (overseas) 50p

No cross on crown £8

No cross on crown and broken frame £25

Aniline scarlet £40

½d Green (half profile by Mackennal). Issued January 1913

Regular Usage, single for Inland rate to 1918 . . . . 5p

Regular Usage, pair for Inland rate from 1918 . . . . 15p

Regular Usage, pair for overseas rate to 1918 . . . . 30p

Regular Usage, single with 1d Mackennal for inland rate 1921–22 . . . . . 20p

New moon flaw £75

1d Red (half profile by Mackennal). Issued October 1912

Regular Usage, overseas rate to 1918 . . . . 15p

Regular Usage, inland rate from 1918 . . . . 5p

Regular Usage, single with ½d Mackennal for inland rate 1921–22 . . . . . 20p

Q for O in 'one' £45

1½d Brown. Issued October 1912

Regular Usage, inland 1921–22 . . . . 30p

PENCF for PENCE £35

British Empire Exhibition, Wembley 1924, 1d Red

First Day Card, 23 April 1924 . . . . £250

Other dates with Wembley Park 1924 slogan cancellation £10

As above but slogans advertising Exhibition not posted Wembley £7.50

As above but other postmarks £5

Tail N to Exhibition £20

British Empire Exhibition, Wembley 1925, 1d Red

First Day Card, 9 May 1925 . . . . £500

Other dates with Wembley Park 1925 slogan cancellation £15
As above but slogans advertising Exhibition, not posted Wembley £10
As above but other postmarks £7.50

Ninth U.P.U. Congress, 1929
First Day Card (any value), 10 May 1929 . . . . £250
Regular Usage, 1d Red 75p
Regular Usage, pair of ½d Green £2

½d Green, Photogravure
First Day Card, (pair), 19 November 1934 . . . . £10
Regular Usage, (pair) 10p

1d Scarlet, Photogravure
First Day Card, 24 September 1934 . . . . £8
Regular Usage 10p

Silver Jubilee, 1935
First Day Card, (½d or 1d), 7 May 1935 . . . . £70
Regular Usage, 1d scarlet 75p
Regular Usage, pair of ½d green 75p

King Edward VIII (1936)
First Day Card (½d or 1d), 1 September 1936 . . . . £3
Regular Usage, 1d scarlet 20p
Regular Usage, pair of ½d green 30p
Regular Usage, ½d green with ½d GV or ½ GVI 30p

King George VI (From 1936)
½d Green
First Day Card, pair, 10 May 1937 . . . . £2.50
Regular Usage, pair 15p
1d Red
First Day Card, 10 May 1937 . . . . £2.50
Regular Usage 10p

POSTAGE DUES Until 1914 surcharges due to underpayment or breaches of regulations were indicated simply by one or more relevant handstamps applied by the office of posting, (see POSTMARK section). Since 1914 the charge has been collected by means of adhesive 'Postage Due' stamps. Charges are generally 'double the deficiency'. Having been neglected for some years postage due stamps neatly tied to card for the purpose for which they were intended are now becoming popular with collectors.

	First Day Card	Regular use on postcard
Watermark George V Royal Cypher (Issued 20 April 1914)		
½d Green	£300	£1.75
1d Red	£200	50p

1½d Brown	£8
2d Black	£1
3d Violet	£1.25

Watermark George V Block Cypher, 1924

½d Green	£1.50
1d Red	50p
1½d Brown	£10
2d Black	£1
3d Violet	£1

Watermark Edward VIII, 1936

½d Green	£5
1d Red	£1.75
2d Black	£1.50
3d Violet	£1.50

Watermark George VI, 1937

½d Green	£3
1d Red	50p
2d Black	50p
3d Violet	50p

Many other varieties and shades can, of course, be found on postcards. These can be found listed in *Stanley Gibbons Stamp Catalogue, Part 1, British Commonwealth* 1983 or, in greater detail, *Stanley Gibbons Great Britain Specialised Stamp Catalogue, Vol.1: Queen Victoria, Vol.2: King Edward VII to King George VI* all published by Stanley Gibbons Publications Ltd, 391 Strand, London, WC2R 0LX.

In addition other types worth looking out for, if only as exceptions to routine, include the following:

1. Government Official Overprints (I. R. Official etc) These are rare because they obviously indicate fraudulent use. Value from £10.

2. Perfins. Stamps with perforated initials of firms. Usually in a similar category to the above. Value £2 though a premium would be warranted if the initials relate to the picture theme of the card.

3. Postal Staionery 'cut-outs'. Value from £2.

4. Re-use. Stamps previously used and then tied to card by a postmark of a different date. Value from £1 whether noticed by G.P.O. and surcharged or not. (Cards with a message but which have not passed through the post and to which a collector has fixed a postmarked stamp are not worth anything from the postal viewpoint.)

5. Poached Egg. G.P.O. Testing Label, accepted as ½d postage in 1936. Value £3.

6. Meter Marks on postcard. Values from 50p.

7. Cards Overpaid presumably because the sender did not have a low value stamp but wanted to post the card urgently. Cards with 1d for ½d and 1½d for 1d may indicate some kind of late fee but higher values such as 3d or 4d are found, if rarely.

THE POSTMARK

Introduction

The Postmark is very useful to the Postcard Collector for it usually provides him with his only firm evidence of date. The Collector can be quite certain that, by the date of the postmark, the card had been designed or photographed, printed and sold but he must remember that cards were often held in stock for many years. For the topographical collector what could be better than to have his viewcard clearly postmarked with a contemporary local postmark? Some postmarks are valuable and it may well be that the interest of a rather undistinguished card is transformed when the significance of its postmark is realised.

Postmark collecting is now a hobby in its own right and recent years have seen significant price rises as many new collectors have become interested. For the postmark collector postcards are often the only available source of the markings of earlier this century for, though cards were often kept for decades in old albums, envelopes were usually thrown away as of no lasting interest.

Over two centuries of development lay behind British postmarks before the birth of the postcard. Until 1840 the function of the postmark was to indicate the place of posting, though other information such as the date and time of posting was sometimes given. The issue of adhesive postage stamps in 1840, the famous Penny Black and Twopenny Blue, necessitated another type of mark – an 'Obliterator' or 'cancellation' to prevent re-use. It was some time before these originally independent functions became fully incorporated into a single postmark, a process not complete by the postcard era.

At first the postage stamp was cancelled by a 'Maltese Cross' or by a numbered obliterator, each Post Office being given a separate number in 1844. Every item of mail continued to receive a despatch datestamp on the reverse. This, however, necessitated two operations and so, from 1853, a double headed or 'duplex' type came into use which lasted in some places until the First War period. In the 1880s the two functions were, for the first time, incorporated together in the 'squared circle' or 'combined obliterator'. Both the squared circle and the duplex have been termed 'killers' by philatelists – the heavy impression they gave was a deliberate precaution against fraudulent re-use. By the early twentieth century squared circles were being gradually replaced by double circles whose thick arcs had the same function as the old killers. Slowly the arcs became thinner and alongside them single circles of various sizes came into use as cancellation marks. The colossal number of postcards sent during the Edwardian era was undoubtedly a major factor in the adoption of mechanised cancellation and by the end of the reign a substantial proportion of the mail was being machine cancelled. Slogans were first used in 1917 to encourage people to support the War effort by buying War Bonds. Many other national campaigns were similarly publicised in the inter-war years.

In the section below a selection of postmarks is given for the first half century of the British postcard, 1890–1940. They are taken from my book *Collect British Postmarks* by Dr J. T. Whitney, B.P.H. Publications, Second Edition 1980 (£5.50 + 55p postage from Picton Publishing). Each section below contains a cross reference to the pages in CBP2 where more detail may be found (e.g. full lists of Duplex numbers, squared circles, T.P.O. marks, paquebot, etc.). All sections in CBP are fully priced according to current market values and there is a bibliography of specialised books on particular types.

Prices are for clear strikes on clean cards, and incomplete marks should be reduced accordingly. Only a very basic listing is given and each type may cover many hundreds, or even thousands, of versions varying in value depending on the length of 'life' of the mark, the area from which it comes, etc. In general, postmarks from small villages will be worth more than those from large towns. Prices are therefore the minimum you would expect to pay for a clear mark of this type.

DUPLEX (CBP2 pp20–45)

Large Post Offices were allocated a number in 1844 and smaller offices were added later. The numbers ran from 1–199 enclosed in a pattern of bars though Scotland and Ireland did not need all the numbers while England and Wales needed more and so supplemented by letter prefixes. In all, five series were issued. From 1853 Duplex types came into use incorporating both numeral and datestamp in a 'double' stamp. Although the numeral part was meant to cancel each stamp on a cover, when more than one was affixed, this rule was largely ignored by the postcard era. Meanwhile the numeral, consisting of six or eight bars, had become taller. Duplex marks were gradually replaced by other types during the reign of George V though the earlier numeral marks contined to be pressed into emergency use when, for example, an item missed cancellation.

Numeral cancellation (without datestamp) on Edward VII stamps £2.50
   As above but George V period £3.50

1 London Inland Section Duplex. Numeral in inner diamond £1.75
   London District Post Duplex. Numeral in inner circle £1.50
2 London Suburban Duplex £1.50
3 England and Wales Duplex. Numeral in oval pattern of bars 50p
   Scottish Duplex. Numeral in square pattern of bars £2.50
   Irish Duplex. Numeral in diamond pattern of bars £3
   Double prices for George V period

SQUARED CIRCLE (CBP2 pp46–57)

The first postmark to incorporate the functions of obliteration and place/date/time of posting into a single headed cancellor. The life of this 'combined obliterator' exactly coincided with the classic postcard age coming into use during the 1890s and disappearing in the twenties. Its chief disadvantage was that the heavy corners tended to

124

cut deeply into covers or postcards. A number of experimental types were used in various parts of London but these are rarely found on postcards with the exception of **4** which was used for mail landed from ships. The regular issue exists in several sizes both with and without indexes.

| 4 | 5 | 6 |

4 Octagonal type without corners from 1902 . . . . £4
5 Regular issue, without index number, Edward VII 40p
   As above but George V 50p
6 Regular issue, with index number, Edward VII 55p
   As above but George V 75p

DOUBLE CIRCLES (CBP2 p59)

These postmarks, first introduced in the 1890s, are the most commonly found of all postcard postmarks. There are many varieties leading directly to the types in use today. This is a cheap field still open to specialisation.

| 7 | 8 | 9 |

7 Double circle with two pairs of arcs broken by office number, mainly
   Scottish towns 75p
8 Double circle with one pair of arcs broken by cross 10p
9 As above but stamp number 15p
   As above but post town, county, etc. 15p
   As above but star £1

SINGLE CIRCLES (CBP2 p58)

First used as backstamps on letters of the 1850s, these postmarks were widely used on postcards. Again there is an immense variety leading to their modern derivative the counterwork handstamp. Sizes vary greatly from the large Irish type (which should not be confused with a 'skeleton') to the 'thimble' so called because if a thimble were placed on it no part of the postmark shows. Single rings were used on postcards in at least three ways: to cancel the stamp, as a receiving mark by the destination P.O. and by a small P.O. alongside the cancellation of its superior office. The first two should be priced normally but the third as at least double because it indicates that this office, often an out-of-the-way hamlet, did not at that time sort its own mail but merely forwarded it on.

10

11

10 Single circles, medium size	. . . .	50p
11 Thimbles	. . . .	75p

MACHINE CANCELLATIONS (CBP2 pp62-71)

The G.P.O. had been experimenting with machine cancellors since one designed by Rowland Hill's son, Pearson Hill, in 1857. The great numbers of postcards posted in Edwardian times led to increased experimentation. From the many tried, three emerged as leaders: Krag, Hey Dolphin and Universal. All this experimentation produced a great variety of strikes before the Universal impression was adopted as standard in 1934. This is therefore a very complicated field including both the cheapest and the dearest postmarks to be found on postcards. Only a few examples can be listed below.

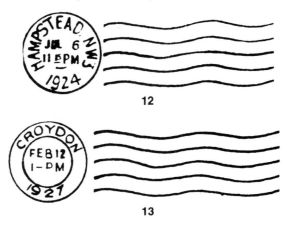

12

13

Hey Dolphin (fixed year at base of datestamp, undulating bars):

12 Single circle datestamp	. . . .	50p
13 Double circle datestamp	. . . .	40p

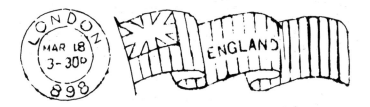

14

Imperial Mail Marking:
14 England Flag, used on four days in March 1898 . . . . £600

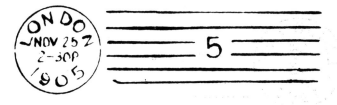

15

Bickerdike:
15 Single circle, E Crown R in straight bars £1

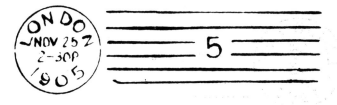

16

Boston:
16 Single circle, code numbers in straight bars £1

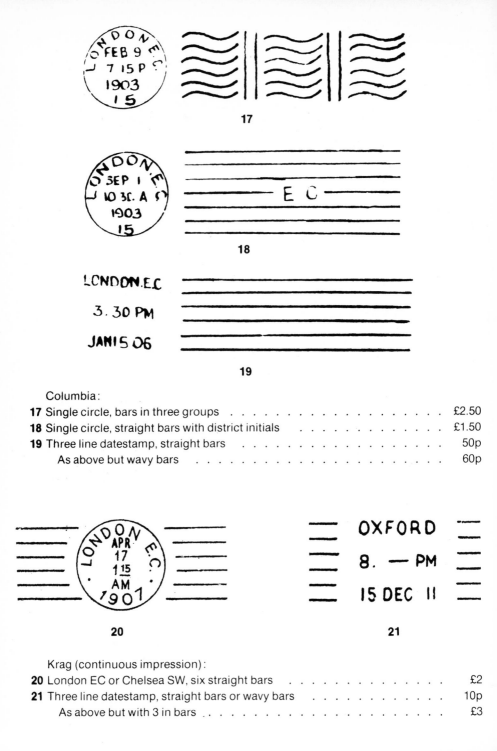

17

18

LONDON.EC

3.30 PM

JAN 15 06

19

Columbia:

17 Single circle, bars in three groups £2.50
18 Single circle, straight bars with district initials £1.50
19 Three line datestamp, straight bars 50p
    As above but wavy bars 60p

20

21

Krag (continuous impression):

20 London EC or Chelsea SW, six straight bars £2
21 Three line datestamp, straight bars or wavy bars 10p
    As above but with 3 in bars £3

 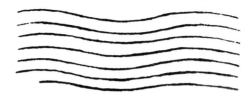

22

Universal:

Croydon double arc	£5
22 Single circle, wavy bars	10p

MACHINES WITH SLOGANS (CBP2 pp72–5)

The familiar slogan first appeared in 1917 to publicise War Bonds. Over a hundred others were used in the period up to the Second War. Only events or causes of national significance were allowed into slogans in this period. Many slogans are still very cheaply available on postcards.

BRITISH GOODS
ARE BEST

23   **24**

23 War Bond types	60p
Wembley Exhibition types	50p
24 British Goods	20p
Post Early Sunburst	20p
British Industries Fair types	50p
Telephone slogans	20p
Christmas slogans	25p
Glasgow Exhibition	20p
King's Roll	£1.50

Among the many other types of postal marking to be found on postcards are the following:

SKELETONS (CBP2 pp58-9)

Large £6
(with spelling mistakes, from £8.50)

Small £6

One line date £5

RUBBERS (CBP2 p58)
(blue black or violet, prices for clear strikes)

£3

With head office across centre £5

Rubber skeleton £15

MIS-SORT (CBP2 p58)

£1

SCROLLS (CBP2 p60)

London £2
Liverpool £3.75
Others from £6

WILKINSON MACHINE (CBP2 p61)

25 Jan or 31 Aug 1912, £15
Other dates £100

DOUBLE RIM (CBP2 p61)

£2

HAMMERS (CBP2 p61)

£40

CORKS

£2

SPECIAL EVENTS (CBP2 pp76–82)

(All commemorative marks
before 1907 are worth at
least £8.50)

1907 Dublin Exhib £5
1908 Edinburgh Exhib £8
1908 Franco-British £1
1908 Ballymaclinton £1.40
1909 Ballymaclinton £4
1909 International Imp £5

1910 Japanese British £4
1910 Ditto machine £12
1911 Crystal Palace £9.50
1911 Coronation Ex. £6
1911 Aerial London £10
1911 Aerial Windsor £16

RAILWAY STATIONS (CBP2 p83)

Duplex Stations £4
Squared circle stations £3
Single circle stations £1.75
Double circle stations £1

RSO Single circles £1
RSO Double circles 50p

TRAVELLING POST OFFICES (CBP2 pp83–112)

Duplex £10
Squared circles £7

Sorting Tenders £6
Double circles £3

Edwardian single circles £5
Georgian single circles £4

MARITIME MARKINGS (CBP2 pp113–32)

Shipletter cds £6
Packet letter cds £8

Paquebot straight lines £4
Paquebot circular types £2
Paquebot machines £1.50

Foreign paquebot on
British Stamps £1.50

| Posted on the High
Seas £6.50
As above but with
ship's name £7 | H & K Packet £25 | Marguerite
– unframed £35
– circular £85
Tudno, Elvies or
Snowdon £175 |

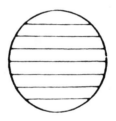

| Columba £25
Iona £35
Grenadier £150
Chevalier £250 | Dumb, Naval
Security £1 | Sea Post Office 75p
Liverpool Sea P.O. £50
Southampton Sea P.O. £80
Transatlantic P.O. £18
Transatlantic Plymouth £100 |

| London MB £9.50
Southampton MB £8.50 | Jersey Octagonal MB £95
Jersey Milestone MB £85 |

WARS (CBP2 pp133–5)

Boer War	First War	Skeleton 50p
Single circles £7	Army P.O. 20p	Machine 30p
Double circles £17.50	Field P.O. 30p	

CAMPS (CBP2 pp136–60)

Duplex £5	Double circle £2	Machine £2
Single circle £2.50		Skeleton £5

ISLANDS (CBP2 pp161–6)

Alderney with cross £13
Sark single ring £15
Herm £300
Jersey and Guernsey:
Head Office 50p
Sub Offices £2

Douglas I.O.M. 50p
Ramsey £1.50
Castletown £5
Peel Duplex £6
Port Erin S.O. £1
Other Offices £5

I.O.W. 40p
Lundy £25
Hayling £3
Holy Island £5
Scottish Isles £1

CHARGE AND INSTRUCTIONAL MARKS (CBP2 pp167–77)

½d £4	½D £3	Liable to Letter rate 75p
1d £1.50	1D 75p	Contrary to Regulations £1
2d £2	2D £1.75	Other T-shaped £1

Letter Rate £1
Postcard Rate £1.20

Taxe Marks £1.50

Foreign Branch or
Inland Section £1

EXAMINATION MARKS (CBP2 pp177)

ROYALTY (CBP2 pp186–7)

75p

All Scarce

CHRISTMAS (CBP2 pp180–5)

Manchester £70
Others from £150

Manchester £50
Others from £75

Christmas Day £1

CACHETS (CBP2 pp189–93)

Land's End 50p
Snowdon £2
Ben Nevis £3

Beachy Head 75p
Snaefell £7

Hotels 50p
Stationers 30p
Northern Belle £50

Overseas Stamps and Postmarks

This is, of course, an even bigger field. It is also one where little study has been published and much remains unknown. The value of the stamp can easily be checked in a relevant stamp catalogue but pricing postmarks is much more difficult. The following comments may be useful.

1. France, Germany, Italy, Belgium, Holland, Switzerland, Spain and Portugal have large populations. 'Routine' postmarks are worth little at present. Similar comments apply to USA and India.

2. Any maritime or railway postmarks will be exceptions to the above.

3. Smaller European countries like Iceland, Andorra, Monaco and Luxemburg are more in demand.

4. Any area where political change has rendered the postmark obsolete is desirable, e.g. Russian postcards of the Tsarist period, postmarks of disputed territorial areas (Poland, Italian Tirol, Romania, etc.).

5. All cards with GB overprints (including Irish Free State overprints) are worth at least £2. British Post Offices in Constantinople, Tangiers, etc. are keenly sought (from £4).

6. Palestine and all Judaica attract many collectors.

7. Latin America is increasing in popularity, especially the smaller states like Haiti, Cuba, Puerto Rico.

8. 'British Europe', Cyprus, Malta and Gibraltar have always been philatically popular.

9. Former European Colonies, e.g. Belgian Congo, Portugese Mozambique, Dutch East India and German Colonies are becoming popular. Liberia and Ethiopia are much more sought than Egypt or Morocco.

10. Market leaders are undoubtedly small British Colonial Islands. Commercially used on postcards these issues are often worth many times more than the catalogue value of the stamp.

You're never too young to learn! at Tunstall, Suffolk. £8

POSTCARD CLUBS

Bradford & District Postcard Society.
A. E. Wood, 26 Front View, Shelf, Halifax, W. Yorkshire, HX3 7JU.

Cambridge Univ. Deltiologists.
M. Ellison, Clare College.

Canal Card Collectors Circle.
A. K. Robinson, 56 Henley Avenue, Dewsbury, W. Yorks.

Canterbury & East Kent Postcard Club.
Jo White, 27 Milton Avenue, Margate, Kent.

Chester & District Postcard Club.
Kathryn Goulborn, 4 Ffordd Pelydryn, Hawarden, Nr. Chester.

Colchester & District Card Collectors Club.
Stephen Andrews, 30 Millers Lane, Stanway, Colchester.

Cotswold Postcard Collectors Club.
Philip Griffiths, 10 Smyth House, The Waterloo, Cirencester, Glos. GL7 2QR.

Dewsbury & District Postcard Society.
Mr R. J. Marsh, 3 Deneside, Kingsway, Ossett, W. Yorks.

Fairground Postcard Society.
Stan White, 57 Stanley Street, Rothwell, Kettering, Northants.

Great Britain, Postcard Club of
Mrs Drene Brennan, 34 Harper House, St. James Crescent, London SW9 7DW.

Herts Postcard Club.
Ron Rundell, 5 Dryden Crescent, Stevenage, Herts.

Huddersfield & District Postcard Society.
Frank Spicer, Suffield Cottage, Moorhead, Gildersome, Leeds LS27 7BA.

Hull & Humberside Postcard Collectors' Society.
Christopher Ketchell, Flat 2, 105 Princes Avenue, Hull, N. Humberside.

Irish Picture Postcard Society.
Cathair Books, T. D. Rose, South Ding Street, Dublin 2.

Leeds Postcard Club.
Mrs A. Whitelock, 9 Brentwood Grove, Leeds, Yorks LS12 2DB.

Lincoln Collectors Club.
P. L. Rowlett, c/o British Legion Club, Broadgate, Lincoln.

London Postcard Club.
Joyce Cohen, 58 Sandringham Road, London NW11.

Maidstone Postcard Clubs.
Mrs I. Hales, 40 Hildenborough Crescent, Maidstone, Kent.

Manx Postcard Association.
Alan E. Kelly, 18 Inner Circle, Brey Hill, Douglas I.O.M.

Mercia Postcard Club.
Maurice L. Palmer, 5 Saxon Rise, Earls Barton, Northants NN6 0NY.

Merseyside Postcard Club.
P. W. Wooley, 7 Patrick Avenue, Bootle L20 6EP.

Moonrakers Postcard Club.
P. Waddingham, 34 Liddingham Way, Trowbridge, Wilts.

Newcastle-upon-Tyne Postcard Club.
F. A. Fletcher, 35 St. George's Terrace, East Boldon, Tyne and Wear NE36 0LU

Norfolk Postcard Club.
P. J. Standley, 63 Folly Road, Wymondham, Norfolk.

Nottingham Postcard Club.
Peter Davies, 19 Fisher Avenue, Woodthorpe, Nottingham.

Northern Ireland Postcard Club.
William J. Nelson, 56b Willow Gardens, Dummuny, Co. Antrim.

North Wales Postcard Club.
Mike Day, 39 Links Avenue, Little Sutton, South Wirral.

Peterborough & District Postcard Club.
Stephen Perry, 68 Sallows Road, Peterborough PE1 4EU.

Pickering Postcard Club.
Mrs B. Hood, 21 St. Peter Street, Norton, Malton.

Royalty Postcard Collectors Club.
Mrs Cindy Morris, 5 Shrubbery Hill, Cookley, Kidderminster, Worcs DY10 3UW.

Rushden Collectors Circle.
Mrs J. Church, 2 Meadow Drive, Higham Ferrers, NN9 8EZ.

Somerset Postcard Club.
Graham Viner, 10 Hartley Cottages, Pilton, Nr. Shepton Mallet, Somerset.

South Devon Postcard Club.
Mike Dadley, Flat 3, 109 Totnes Road, Paignton, Devon.

Southampton & District Postcard & Cigarette Card Collectors Club.
Tony Pritchard, 96 Rosebery Avenue, Hythe, Hants SO4 6GZ.

Southern Africa Postcard Research Group.
A. K. W. Atkinson, Westcroft, The Crofts, Castletown, I.O.M.

Suffolk Postcard & Cigarette Card Club.
Cliff Weston, 'Galena', Grove Road, Bentley, Ipswich, Suffolk.

Surrey Postcard Club.
Simon Burke, 7 Sandfield Terrace, Guildford, Surrey.

Sussex Postcard Club.
Dave Bull, 12 The Broadway, Lancing.

Tayside, Postcard Club of
Sydney Mitchell, 36 Bruce Road, Dundee DD3 8LL.

Tees Valley Collectors Club.
Joan Lambert, 24 Beechwood Avenue, Darlington, Co. Durham.

Wyre Forest Postcard Club.
Derek Gallimore, The Grange, 30 Pinewoods Avenue, Hagley, Stourbridge, W. Midlands.

Notice to Society Secretaries If Secretaries will write to us with details of new societies and changes of personnel and/or addresses we will publish them in the next edition.

The Mail Motor at Winforten near Hay, Hereford. £25

SOME MAGAZINES FOR
THE PICTORIAL POSTCARD COLLECTOR

MODERN POSTCARD MAGAZINES

1. *Postcard World* Organ of the Postcard Club of Great Britain published by Mrs D. Brennan, 34 Harper House, St James' Crescent, Brixton, London SW9 7LW.

2. *Transy News* published by H. Richardson, 27B Marchmont Road, Edinburgh EH9 1HY.

3. *Picture Postcard Monthly* published by B & M Lund, 27 Walton Drive, Keyworth, Notts.

4. *The Exchange and Mart,* Link House, Dingwall Avenue, Croydon CR9 2TA. It contains only advertisements but has a 'Picture Postcard' section.

5. *La Cartophile,* organ of the Cercles Français des Collectioneurs des Cartes Postales, 117 Bd. Saint Germain, Paris 6, France. (Open to membership application).

6. *The British Postcard Collector's Magazine,* Ron Griffiths, 47 Long Arrotts, Hemel Hempstead MP1 3EX.

7. *Finders Keepers,* Kollectorama, Bembridge, Isle of Wight.

SOME HANDBOOKS TO HELP THE COLLECTOR
OF GOVERNMENT PRODUCED POSTCARDS

Higgins & Gage – *Priced Catalogue of Postal Stationery of the World,* G.B. Section, 1967 is Part 7 – Pasadena, California, USA.

Huggins, A.K. – *British Postal Stationery,* published by the Great Britain Philatelic Society, 1970.

SELECT BIBLIOGRAPHY

SOME MAINLY MODERN BOOKS TO HELP THE POSTCARD COLLECTOR

Alderson, F. – *The Comic Postcard in English Life,* 1970.

Alsop, J. (with Wright, I. and Hilton, B.) A series of twenty booklets on Official Railway Postcards.

Andrews, B. – *A Directory of Postcards, Artists, Publishers and Trademarks* an American production covering the world, 1975.

Baudet, Annie & Francois, *Nouvelle Encyclopedie Illustrée Internationale de la Carte Postale* Vols 1 and 2.

Bernard, I. and W. – *Picture Postcard Catalogue – Germany 1870–1945* priced, in English, French and German, current.

Special Picture Postcard Catalogue – National Socialism 1933–45 priced, in English, French and German, 1976.

Buday, George, A.R.E. – *The Story of the Christmas Card* Odhams Press Ltd, London, 1951.

Burdick, J.R. – *Pioneer Postcards* the story of mailing cards to 1898 with an illustrated check list of publishers and titles. Whole world, reprinted recently, originally printed 1956.

Butland, A.J. and Westwood, E.A. - *Picture Postcards and All about Them* printed by Rutherdale Stationery Co Ltd, Teddington, Middlesex. Includes the first G.B. priced catalogue of pictorial postcards of modern times, 1959.

Byatt, A. - *Picture Postcards and their Publishers*, 1978.

Calder-Marshal, A. - *The Art of Donald McGill* selected and appraised by, 1966.

Campbell, G. and Schoeller, A. - *Catalogue des Cartes Postales (1889)* in French.

Cane, Michael - *For Queen & Country, (The Career of Harry Payne)*, 1977.

Carline, Richard - *Pictures in the Post* (1959) Gcrdon Frazer Ltd. Bedford. (Revd. Ed. 1971). Contains a fine bibliography at the commencement of the book.

Carver, Sally S. - *Tuck* American postcard guide to Tuck cards, Massachusetts, 1976.

Cope, Dawn & Peter - *Illustrators of Postcards from the Nursery*, 1978.

Duval, W. & Monahan, Valerie - *Collecting Postcards in Colour* Blandford Press, Dorset, 1978, Pt 2 1914-30, 1980.

Evans, Jane - *Ivy Millicent James 1879-1965* Woodspring Museum, Weston-super-Mare, 1980.

Fildier, Argus - *Cartes Postales Anciennes de Collection* (annually) fine French catalogue - priced. French scene.

Filnkobl, H. *100 Jahre Postkarte*, 1973.

Fletcher, F.A. and Brooks, A.D. - *British Exhibitions and Their Postcards. Part 1 1900-1914, Part 2 1915-1979*

Frech, H. - *Private Postcard Catalogue* in German, priced - special events, c.1975.

Freeman, L. Dr. - *Wish you were here* Century House, New York 14891, 1976.

Fumagalli, Luigi - *Catalogo Internazionale delle Cromo-Litografie Liebig* (Fada). Third edition with supplements 1957. Fully priced, deals with all the Liebig trade cards.

Guyonnet, George - *La Carte Postale Illustrée. Son Histoire, Sa Valeur Documentaire.* edited by the Chambre Syndicale Française de la Carte Postale Illustrée, c.1946. The French scene.

Hammond, P. - *French Undressing*, 1976.

Hill, C. W. - *Discovering Picture Postcards* Shire Publications, Tring, 1970.

Holt, Valmai and Tonie - *Picture Postcards of the Golden Age, Collectors' Guide* Fine production, 1971.

— *Till the Boys come Home: The Picture Postcards of the First World War* published by Macdonald & Jane's, 1977.

Kaduck, J.M. - *Mail Memories (Pictorial Guide to Postcard Collecting)* with prices, highly illustrated, American scene, 1971.

Lawrence, P.N. - *Picture postcard 1870-1920* a brochure relating to the travelling exhibition arranged by the Circulation Dept. of the Victoria and Albert Museum of Postcards contributed to the exhibition by the author, Mr P.N. Lawrence.

— *The Social Significance of the Picture Postcard*, 1975.

Lauterbach & Jokovsky - *A Picture Postcard Album,* published by Thames & Hudson, 1961.

Lawson, K. & Warr, A. - *The Postcards of Tom Browne,* Postcards for Pleasure, 1978.

— *The Postcards of Lance Thackery,* Postcards for Pleasure 1978.

Lowe, J.L. & Papell, B. – *Detroit Publishing Company Collectors' Guide,* 1975.

— *Standard Postcard Catalogue,* Better Postcard Collectors' Club, Gradyville, P.A., USA. First Edition 1968.

Lowe, J.L. – *Lincoln Postcard Catalogue, 1967* all the cards associated with President Lincoln, priced.

Mackay, James A. – *Scottish Postmarks* 11 Newhall Terrace, Dumfries, 1978.

Miller, D. and G. – *Picture Postcards in the United States 1893–1918* Clarkson N. Potter, New York, 1976.

Mobbs, Ann – *The Cat Fancier, Longman 1982* – A guide to Cat Postcards.

Mucha, Ira – *The Graphic Work of Alphonse Mucha,* Academy Editions, 1973.

Neudin, J. – *Cartes Postales de Collection* a fine annual catalogue (in French), priced, French scene.

O'Reilly, Patrick – *Centenaire de la Carte Postale (1871–1970),* 1970.

Quellete, W. – *Fantasy Postcards* 1975.

Pictons Catalogue 1981 – *Harry Payne Postcards.*

Pictons Catalogue 1982 – Coloured Railway Postcards.

Radley, C. – *History of Silk Postcards* first listing of embroidered cards as well as woven – scarcity graded 1975.

— *Collecting Silk Postcards* 1976.

— *Embroidered Silk Postcards* 1977.

— *The Woven Silk Postcard* 1978.

Scott, W.J. – *All about Postcards 1903* a fine *contemporary* handbook in the hey-day of the *Edwardian* postcard craze.

Scherer, R.W. – *Bamforth Checklist* Parts 1 and 2, 1973.

Silvester, J. – *Official Railway Postcards of the British Isles, Pt1, LNWR* BPH Publications, 1978.

— *Official Railway Postcards of the British Isles, Pt2, GWR and Others* BPH Publications, 1981.

Smith, J. (I.P.M.) – *Catalogue of Picture Postcards and Year Book.* A fine catalogue by an eminent British dealer, an 'annual' production.

Sprake, A.M.A. and Darby, M. – *Stevengraphs* 1968, printed by Fletcher & Son Ltd., Norwich and the priced guide of 1971.

Staff, Frank – *The Picture Postcard and its Origins* 1966, Lutterworth Press, a most erudite production, highly recommended and also for the philatelically inclined (reprinted 1979).

— *The Valentine and its Origins* 1969.

Weill, Alan – *Art Nouveau Postcards* Thames & Hudson Ltd, 1977.

Welsh, Roger, L. – *Tall-Tale Postcards* A.S. Barnes & Co, New Jersey 08512, 1976.

Whitney, Dr J.T. – *Collect British Postmarks* (2nd Edition 1980) Picton Publishing.

Wolstenholme, George – *ABC of Postcard Collecting* 1973.

— *Peeps into the Postcard Past* 1974.

N.B. Most of the *catalogues* listed above are repeated at intervals (not always annually) so check for the latest date when buying.

Authors, editors or publishers, please advise us of any titles suitable for listing, if space allows, in future editions.

LIST OF POSTCARD DEALERS

Code: A, Postal Business; B, Retail Premises; C, Appointment Only; D, Sales List; E, Auction; F, Topographical; G, Subject; H, Modern; J, Postal History; K, Accessories; L, PTA Member.

In addition, the majority of the following dealers trade at fairs and markets and a few at fairs only. We recommend prospective callers to phone before visiting as we are unable to list shop opening days and hours, nor have we any knowledge of the size and quality of stocks.

Abel, Daphne, 11 Nevill Road, Hove, Sussex. Tel. 0423 55430	FGL
Airey, J.F., 6 Wolveleigh Terrace, Gosforth, Newcastle-on-Tyne. Tel. Gosforth 853847	AFL
Antiquardus Company Limited, 5 Buckingham Road, Alexandra Park, London N22 Tel 01 888 6998	ADFGHJ
Armfield, Grace K, 3 Percival Road, Orpington, Kent BR6 8HL Tel. Farnborough 57975	AFG
Athene Postcards Ltd, 22 Cambridge Grove, Hammersmith W6 Tel 01 741 3653	AGL
Bartholomew, Mary, Hastings Antique & Art Centre, 21 White Rock, Hastings, East Sussex. Tel. Hastings 439064	ABFG
Bath Collectors' Centre, Brian Swallow, Great Western Antique Centre, Bartlett Street, Bath, Avon. Tel. 038082 508	BFGJL
The Bath Stamp and Coin Shop, Pulteney Bridge, Bath, Avon BA2 4AY Tel. 0225 63073	
Benarth Stamps, 5 Marsh Lane, Penkridge, Stafford ST19 5BY Tel. 078571 3072	ACDJ
Branch Two, 36 Queens Road, Brighton, Sussex. Tel. 0273 24827	BFGL
Buckley, Bill and Read, Prue, 19 Broad Street, Old Portsmouth PO1 2JD Tel. Portsmouth 814 992	
Bunny Antiques, Chris and Marjorie Vaughan-Jones, 'Lynton', Bunny Hill, Costock, Nr. Loughborough, Leicester. Tel. Leicestershire 050982 2128	ACFJ
Burton Collectors' Centre, D. and R. Matthews, 24 Derby Street, Burton-on-Trent, Staffordshire. Tel. 0283 48494	ABEFGJKL
Cardmania, Wayward, Church Road, Pamber Heath, Nr. Basingstoke, Hants. Tel. 0734 700674	FGL
Carey, Aubrey A., 121 Lordswood Road, Harborne, Birmingham B17 9BH Tel. Birmingham 021 427 4506	
Case, Morley, 144 Western Avenue, Bournemouth BH10 6HL Tel. Northbourne 2573	ACFGJ

Chamberlain, Desmond, PO Box 725, London SW15 3RH Tel. 01 549 0440   AGJL

Chamberlain, Keith, 43 Cumberland Road, Angmering Village, West   ACFGKL
Sussex. Tel. Rustington 09062 6942

Collector Cards, Severn Villa, Coleham Head, Shrewsbury, Salop SY3 7BJ   ABFGL
Tel. 0743 53092

Collectors Mail Auctions (Pty) Limited, PO Box 20, Bergvliet 7864, South   E
Africa.

Collector's World Limited, 28 North Gyle Drive, Edinburgh 12   FGK
Tel. 031 339 5593

Collins, Parktop, St. Albans Road, Ventnor, IOW PO38 1DE

Cox, Michael, Southview, Ipswich Road, Brantham, Manningtree, Essex.
Tel. 020639 3973

Crest Collectors Centre, Mid-Kent Shopping Centre, Allington, Maidstone,   ABFGHJKL
Kent. Tel. Maidstone 52011

Cumbria Postcards, Peter Howarth, 'Hadleigh', 24 Silchester Road, Pamber   ADFGK
Heath, Nr. Basingstoke, Hants RG26 6EE Tel. Silchester 700044

Delta, M. Glasby-Baldwin, 6 Parkside Road, Cornholme, Todmorden, Lancs   FGK
OL14 8PF Tel. 070681 2707

Dendelti, Bob and Betty Roberts, 44 Vale Street, Upper Gornal, Dudley,   FGJ
West Midlands DY3 3XF Tel. 09073 4372

Discards, J & B Alsop, 3 Manorbier Road, Bedford. Tel. 0234 43463   TGL

Ducal, 228a Shirley Road, Southampton, Hants. Tel. 0703 38766   ABFGHJKL

Edge B., 48 Woodside Avenue, Wistaston, Crewe, Cheshire CW2 8AN   CFG
Tel. 0270 69839

Edinburgh Stamp Shop, 91 Leith Walk, Edinburgh EH8 9PP   BFGKL
Tel. 031 554 7028

Edwardian Postcards, Cleve Hill, Cheltenham, Glos   FG
Tel. Cheltenham 672871

Fell, Richard S., 13 Crane Way, Whitton, Middx. Tel. 01 240 1766   FGJL

Francis J. Field Limited, Sutton Coldfield, West Midlands B73 6BJ   ACGJ
Tel. 021 354 1748

'Follies', Harold and Melody Carlton, Stalls M6–M7, Antiquarius, 135 King's   BGK
Road, London SW3 Tel. 01 352 1129

Fryer, Douglas J., 8 Malling street, Lewes, Sussex. Tel. 07916 5959   ABFGHJK

Gazebo, Top Floor, Flea Market, Pierpont Row, Camden Passage, Angel,   B
Islington, London Tel. 01 226 6627

Gems, Eric and Betty White, 11 Rectory Grove, Leigh-on-Sea, Essex.   ABFGJ
Tel. South Benfleet 53835

George, Brian, 65 New Street, St. Neots, Huntingdon, Cambs.

Ginley, T. G., 5 Cottontree Lane, Colne, Lancs BB8 7BB Tel. 0282 861069

Golden Age Postcards, Tony Byatt, 'Valldemosa', 28 St. Peter's Road,   ADFGL
Malvern, Worcs.

Graham, Conrad Dr. 23 Rotherwick Road, London NW11 7DG   E
Tel. 01 455 5080

Griffiths, Ron, 47 Long Arrotts, Hemel Hempstead, Herts HP1 3EX   ADFGH
Tel. Hemel Hempstead 59019

Harris, Valerie, 27 Craven Terrace, London W2. Tel. 01 262 7824   BGL

Hendon Collectors' Centre, Clive Smith, 1 Newark Parade, Greyhound Hill,   FGL
Hendon, London NW4 Tel. 01 203 1772

H.L.B. Antiques, 940 Christchurch Road, Bournmouth Tel. 429252   ABFGJ

IPM Limited, 126 South Street, Dorking, Surrey RH5 4NX Tel. 0306 86008   BCFGL

James, Norwich Auctions Ltd, 33 Timberhill, Norwich NR1 3RL   BEFGJK
Tel. 0603 24817

Jeremy's, The Oxford Stamp Centre, 98 Cowley Road, Oxford   BFGJK
Tel. Oxford 41011

Jubilee Postcards, David Rayner, 25 Arlington Way, Sadlers Wells, London   B
EC1 Tel. 01 837 3101

Judaica Postcards, 110 Park Road, Hale, Cheshire WA15 9JT   ACFGJK
Tel. 061 980 7070

KQ Cards, Ian M. Keen, 3 Montagu Road, Datchet, Nr. Windsor, Berks   ACDFG
Tel. Slough 41773 (Home No.)

King, Norman, 24 Dinting Road, Glossop, Derbyshire. Tel. Glossop 2946   ADEFGJ

Kirkland, Bill, Todwell House, 6 Todwell Lane, Little Horton, Bradford, West   ACFGJKL
Yorkshire BD5 0PR Tel. Bradford 578530

Langley, Arthur, 516 Hornsey Road, London N19. Tel. 01 272 3256   FGL

Langton, Garnet, Burlington Arcade, Bournemouth. Tel. 0202 22352   BFGJ

Lee, Roger, 35 Lister Street, Rotherham Tel. 0709 64012   ACFGJK

Legg, Faith, The Guildhall Bookroom, Church St, Eye, Suffolk.   BFGJ
Tel. Eye 870193

Loton, Graham, 5 Wild Hill, Essendon, Herts. Tel. Potters Bar 42679   FG

Magda Coin Co., PO Box 32, Southend-on-Sea, Essex. Tel. 587603   CFGKL

Manor Antiques, Chris Hoskins, 75a Manor Road, Wallington   ABFGL
Tel. 01 669 5970

N & H Mathews, Harrogate Postcard Shop, 38a Cold Bath Rd, Harrogate.

May, Philip, 22 Hyde Road, Paignton, South Devon TQ4 5BY   BFGK
Tel. 0803 558273

Meads Antiques, S. and T. Partridge, 9 Meads Street, Eastbourne, East   ABFG
Sussex. Tel. 638914

Midland Stamp Company, PO Box 11529, Memphis, TN38111, U.S.A.
Tel. 901 458 3911

Murray Cards International, 51 Watford Way, Hendon, London NW4   BFGKL
Tel. 01 202 5688

Neales of Nottingham, 192 Mansfield Road, Nottingham NG1 3HY   EL
Tel. 0602 624141

Nevitsky, Philip, 191 Manchester Road, Rochdale. Tel. 0706 58266   G

Newcastle on Tyne Postcard Centre, M. Gair, 69 St George's Terrace,   ABCFGHJK
Newcastle on Tyne NE2 2DL Tel. 0632 812831

Old Things (C. Joyce), 1 Spring Lane, Woodside, London SE25   ABFGL

Pandora, W. Musgrove, New Street Antiques Centre, 27 New Street,   ABDFGJ
Barbican, Plymouth, Devon. Tel. Plymouth 61165

Past Delights, 1 Chapel Street, Guildford, Surrey GU1 3UH Tel. 0483 39595   ABFGHJKL

Patzert, Mrs A.O., 49 Queens Road, Mumbles, Swansea. Tel. 61976   FBL

Pettrick, George, 17 Roslyn Avenue, Netherton, Huddersfield, Yorkshire.   FG
Tel. 0484 661648

Phillips, 7 Blenheim Street, New Bond Street, London W1Y 0AS   E
Tel. 01 629 6602

Pleasures of Past Times, 11 Cecil Court, St Martin's Lane, London WC2   BFG
Tel. 01 836 1142

Postcards Etc., H. & R. Nadler, PO Box 4318, Thousand Oaks, California
91359, U.S.A.

Presland's, PO Box 38, Basingstoke, Hants RG21 2BE Tel. 0256 781744   ABFGJKL

Raven Antiques, 256 Lee High Road, London SE13 Tel. 01 852 5066   BFGL

'Recollections', 2 Monkville Parade, Temple Fortune, London NW11   ABL
Tel. 01 458 1026

Reflections of a Bygone Age, Brian and Mary Lund, 27 Walton Drive,   ACDFGHJL
Keyworth, Nottingham Tel. 06077 4087

Reminiscences Limited, 188 Long Lane,Halesowen, West Midlands   ABFGHK
Tel. 021 550 0229

Rigdon, Walter, Stand K-5, Antiquarius, 131 King's Road, London SW3   ABFGL

Robinson, Jean, 676 Blackburn Road, Astley Bridge, Bolton BL1 7AD   ACF
Tel. 0204 51161 also Bolton Thursday Antique Market, St Paul's Parochial
Hall, Newnham Street, Astley Bridge, Bolton, Lancs

RF Postcards, 17 Hilary Crescent, Rayleigh, Essex SS6 8NB   CFGJKL
Tel. 0268 743222

Salisbury Stamp Centre, 53 Fisherton Street, Salisbury, Wiltshire.
Tel. 0722 27781

L. Saunders, 6a Cardigan House, Waterloo Road, Winton, Bournemouth.   BEFGJK
Tel. 0202 513771

Scene Before, E. McKercher, PO Box 23, Bedford MK41 8BR   ADFGJK
Tel. 0234 41524

Scott, Patrick, 118 Manchester Road, Haslingden, Rossendale, Lancs.   ABFG
Tel. 213087

Shakeshaft, S.D., Chapel Collectors Centre, Church Hill, Castor, Nr.   ABFGJK
Peterborough, Cambs. Tel. 0733 263328

Shelron Auctions Ltd, 17 Market Buildings Arcade, Maidstone, Kent.   E
Tel. 54702

Shelron Postcards, 18 New Road, Abbey Wood, London SE2   AFGHJKL

Smith, Howard, 2 West Close, Felpham, Bognor Regis PO22 7LQ   ACDFGJ

Smith, Jill, 21 Darlington Gardens, Shirley, Southampton SO1 5HH   ACFGJL
Tel. 0703 779877

Solent City Postcards, PO Box 24, Fareham, Hants PO15 5LH   AFGJL

Solent Enterprise, 2 Fourways, Church Hill, West End, Southampton SO3 3AU Tel. 04218 4862   FGKL

Something in View, 1 Colonnade House, High Street, Worthing BN11 1NZ Tel. 0903 36201

South Eastern Philatelic Auctions of Cranbrook, Kent. Tel. 0580 211661

Specialised Postcard Auctions, 12 Suffolk Road, Cheltenham. Tel. 0242 580323   EL

Stacocards, Arthur Terry, 204 Malpas Road, Brockley, London SE4   ADFGJ

Stubbs, K., 49 Hamilton Drive, Harold Wood, Romford, Essex   ACFGL

The Stamp Shop, Ray and Christine Shapland, 13 Cross Street, Barnstaple, North Devon. Tel. 0271 5581   ABFGHJKL

The Stamp Shop, 34 St Nicholas Cliff, Scarborough, North Yorkshire YO11 2ES   ABFGJK

Stanley Gibbons International, 391 Strand, London WC2R 0LX Tel. 01 836 8444   ABFGJK

Stannard, Peter, PO Box 29, Bognor Regis, West Sussex PO21 5UH

Strathearn Antiques & Curios, 2 Comrie Street, Crieff, Perthshire, Scotland. Tel. Crieff 4344   BFGJK

Sturge, Mike, 17 Market Buildings Arcade, Maidstone, Kent. Tel. Maidstone 54702   ABEFGJK

Tait, Lynn, 85a Chalkwell Esplanade, Westcliff-on-Sea, Essex. Tel. 0702 713347   FG

Taylor, Sylvia, 43 Saxonbury Avenue, Sunbury-on-Thames, Middlesex.   FG

Transy News, H. Richardson, 27b Marchmont Road, Edinburgh EH9 1HY Tel. 031 229 8043   ABDFGJL

Tonge, Alan, 70 Birch Road, Rixton, Warrington WA3 6JS   FG

Trotter, John, 16 Brockenhurst Gardens, London NW7 Tel. 01 959 7615

Vale Stamps, 21 Tranquil Vale, Blackheath, London SE3 0BU Tel. 01 852 9817   B

Vera Trinder Limited, 38 Bedford Street, Strand, London WC2E 9EU Tel. 01 836 2365/6   K

Vintage Postcards, 14 Wheatlands, Hounslow TW5 0SA Tel. 01 570 7458   ACDFGJL

Wax 'n' Wicks, 15 St Lawrence Lane, Ashburton, Devon. Tel. 0364 52855   B

West End Stamp Company, 23 Needless Alley, Birmingham 2

West London Auctions, Sandringham Mews, High Street, Ealing, London W5 Tel. 01 567 6215/7096

White, Ian, 3 Fitzwilliam Place, Dublin 2, Ireland.

Winchester Stamp Centre, 6 Parchment Street, Winchester, Hants Tel. 0962 62491   ABFGJKL

Winter, Tim and Jackie, 8 Weysprings, Haslemere, Surrey GU27 1DE   AFG
Tel. Haslemere 2379

Wiseman, Neville, 605 Lytham Road, Blackpool. Tel. 0253 43471

Wolstenholme, George, 13 Westroyd Park, Mirfield, Yorkshire.   AD
Tel. 0924 493471

Woolley, Eric and Wynn, 14 Beach Road, Bilston, West Midlands WV14 6QF   CFG
Tel. Bilston 45444

A new category for the catalogue –
Parachute Accident, at least £10

A very nice subject/topographical card £6

151

POSTCARDS WANTED

Temperance Movement	Band of Hope Rallies, Motto Cards, Rechabite Banners, Satirical, etc.
Lord's Prayer	Sets or singles.
Hadleigh, Essex	All types, all dates. I pay £1 each for all views except the church and the castle. (My wife's got the postcard bug. *Please* send me some cards and relieve my domestic problems!)
Holy Land	All used cards, all dates.

Look though your rubbish! I will buy **ALL CLEAR POSTMARKS**. Especially TPO, Maritime, Camp, etc. But also **10p each paid** for routine squared circles, duplex, single and double circles, *if clear.* **All foreign postmarks** also wanted. Cash in on your unwanted cards **NOW** and help pay for your hobby.

DR J. T. WHITNEY

75 Church Road, Hadleigh, Benfleet, Essex SS7 2DR

The definitive work on

Isle of Man

Stamps & Postal History

BY DR J. T. WHITNEY

Limited Edition

300 pages and over 1,100 illustrations

published March 1981

BPH PUBLICATIONS

CITADEL WORKS · BATH RD · CHIPPENHAM

WILTSHIRE · SN15 2AB

£20.00

PICTON PUBLISHING
Citadel Works, Bath Road, Chippenham, Wilts SN15 2AB

SHIPS ON STAMPS *by E. W. Argyle*   **£2.00* each**
One: The Royal Navy. **Two**: Passenger Liners. **Three**: Early Sailing Ships and Canoes. **Four**: Sailing Ships. **Five**: Local Craft. **Six**: Cross-Channel, River & Lake Passenger Ships. **Seven**: Cargo Ships, Oil Tankers. **Eight**: Sail & Paddle Auxiliary Vessels. **Nine**: Ships of the World's Navies. **Ten**: Miscellaneous Vessels, Index. **Eleven**: The Royal Navy (New Issues). **Twelve**: Passenger Liners of the World over 4,000 tons.

MUSIC ON STAMPS *by Sylvester Peat*   **£2.00*,each**
One: A–B, Bach, Beethoven, Berlioz and Bartok. **Two**: C–F, Chopin, Debussy, Dvorak and Elgar. **Three**: G–L, Grieg, Handel, Haydn and Liszt. **Four**: M–R, Mahler, Mendlesson, Mozart and Ravel. **Five**: S–Z, Schubert, Sibelius, Strauss and Tchaikovsky. **Six**: Musical Monarchs and National Anthems. **Seven**: Native and Folk Instruments.

Now available, a new series
MORE MUSICIANS ON STAMPS Parts 1 & 2   **£2.00* each**

ISLE OF MAN STAMPS AND POSTAL HISTORY (YPM 4) *by Dr J. T. Whitney*   **£20.00† each**
This is the first handbook to cover all aspects of the philately of this fascinating island. Part One 'The Postal History' contains about 1,000 illustrations, many of them never before published. Part Two 'The Stamps' has illustrations of all the major issues and examples of those used in Local Delivery Services, Strike Posts, etc. This is a *priced* catalogue enabling you to acurately value your collection, but it is also a work of scholarship which has become the standard reference book on the subject frequently quoted by authorities such as Stanley Gibbons. Sized 210 x 148 mm and casebound with 300 pages, no Isle of Man philatelist can afford to be without this work.

COLLECT BRITISH POSTMARKS Second Edition *by Dr J. T. Whitney*   **£5.50† each**
This is the only publication which lists and prices the whole field of British Postal Markings. In this new edition prices have been adjusted in line with current values and there are many new sections and features including coverage of Scottish and Irish postmarks.

THE GREAT RAIDS *by Air Commodore J. H. Searby, DSO DFC*
A series of books on the raids by RAF Bomber Command during World War II. Each book in the series contains information and documents not before published, a complete list of the squadrons and crews who took part and is written superbly by an expert on the subject. He was there.
Part One: PEENEMUNDE. Soft Cover £4.50† Library Edition £7.50†
Part Two: ESSEN. THE BATTLE OF THE RUHR. Soft Cover £5.50† Library Edition £7.50†

TERRIERS IN THE TRENCHES The History of the Post Office Rifles *by Charles Messenger* £12.95†
THE RIFLE VOLUNTEERS 1859–1908 *by Ray Westlake* £9.95†
HEADDRESS, BADGES AND EMBELLISHMENTS OF THE ROYAL CORPS OF SIGNALS
by Major A. G. Harfield £3.00*
ISLANDERS DEPORTED *by Roger Harris*
The story of the Channel Islanders deported to Germany during WWII. £4.20†
ADMIRAL SEYMOUR'S EXPEDITION & TAKU FORTS 1900 *by Colin Narbeth* £7.50†
THE DISTINGUISHED SERVICE MEDAL 1939–1946 *by W. H. Fevyer* £20†
BRITISH GALLANTRY AWARDS 2nd Edition *by P. E. Abbott & J. Tamplin* £18●
1933 CENTENARY ISSUE OF THE FALKLAND ISLANDS *by R. N. Spafford* £5†
PRE-VICTORIAN STAMPS AND FRANKS *by Hewlett & Picton-Phillips* £4† *(new edition)*
THE WHALE'S TALE *by Frederick P. Schmitt* £3.50†
PRINTERS AND PRINTING IN PHILATELY *by John Alden* £3.50†
OFFICIAL RAILWAY POSTCARDS OF THE BRITISH ISLES: Part 1 L&NWR £4* **Part 2** GWR and Others £6*
RAILWAYS ON STAMPS *by A. M. Goodbody and C. A. Hart* £2.00* each
PICTON'S PHILATELIC HANDBOOK No. 1 £4.00†
A CORSHAM BOYHOOD: The Diary of Herbert Spackman 1877–1891
by Faith Sharp with Heather Tanner and illustrations by Robin Tanner £5.95†
THE CURSE OF MACBETH & OTHER THEATRICAL SUPERSTITIONS *by Richard Huggett* £7.95†
FRENCH ISLANDS A Priced Catalogue to the Postal History of the Islands of the North & West Coasts of France
by O. W. Newport & J. T. Whitney £9.95†
THE STAMPS OF ALDERNEY Illustrated Priced Guide & Handbook *by P. Kelley & P. E. Newell* £3.50*
ROADWAYS The History of Swindon's Street Names *by Peter Sheldon & Richard Tomkins* £2.95*
SWINDON IN CAMERA A Photographic Journey 1850–1979 *by Peter Sheldon* £4.50*

Postage and Packing
*=55p †=£1.00 ●=£1.50

These titles available direct from PICTON PUBLISHING or your local bookseller.
Please send SAE (6" x 8½") for free catalogue of all titles.

160

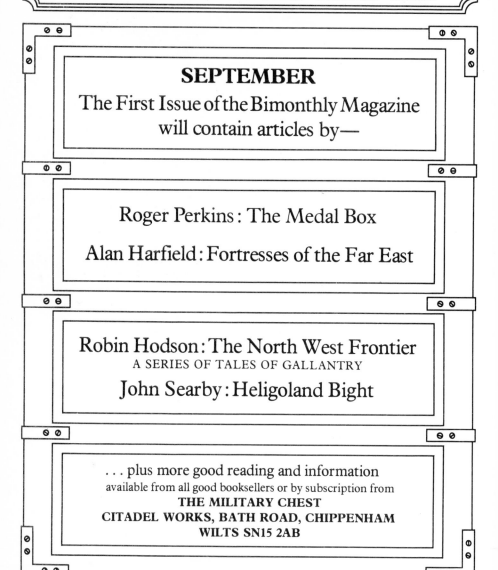

The Military Chest 95p

THE ARMED FORCES, PAST, PRESENT ... AND FUTURE
MILITARY HISTORY • RESEARCH • MEDALS AND INSIGNIA
WEAPONS • NEWS & VIEWS • LETTERS • DEALERS • BOOKS

SEPTEMBER

The First Issue of the Bimonthly Magazine
will contain articles by—

Roger Perkins: The Medal Box

Alan Harfield: Fortresses of the Far East

Robin Hodson: The North West Frontier
A SERIES OF TALES OF GALLANTRY
John Searby: Heligoland Bight

... plus more good reading and information
available from all good booksellers or by subscription from
THE MILITARY CHEST
CITADEL WORKS, BATH ROAD, CHIPPENHAM
WILTS SN15 2AB

IPM Promotions *present*

POSTCARDS ● STAMPS ● CIGARETTE CARDS
● PRINTED EPHEMERA ●

every month at the biggest Postcard Fair on earth! The Bloomsbury Fair has become a legend in its time. Every month since December 1977 up to 150 postcard dealers from all over the British Isles, with many regular dealers from France and Belgium, gather together at Bloomsbury to present their combined stocks to well over 1000 buyers. If you collect postcards then Bloomsbury is the only place to be. It is where it all happens. A monthly get-together of all sections of the postcard world...Dealers...Auctioneers...Publishers...Collectors etc. No matter what you collect in postcards, Topographical or Subjects, Old or Modern, you will find it at Bloomsbury. And find it in quantity — for there are estimated to be over ½ million cards on display at any Bloomsbury Fair.

Held in the magnificent 12,000 sq. ft. exhibition area of this luxury hotel, the Bloomsbury is the international market place for everyone interested in picture postcards.

Regular dealers at Bloomsbury include all the big names in postcards: Pat Presland, Keith Chamberlain, Daphne Abel, Ron Mead & Joan Venman, Bill & Irene Williams, Desmond Chamberlain, IPM, Betty & Bob Roberts, Brian Lund, Dave & Kathy Marmion, Chris Hoskins, Martin Murray, Michael Steyn, Jack & Thelma Duke, Rosina Stevens, Branch Two, Ray Shapland, Chris Easton, Edouard Pecourt, Eric McKercher, Jack Stasiak, Clive Smith, Mike Sturge, Ron Grosvenor, Ken Lawson and many, many more.

WE ALSO RUN OCCASIONAL POSTCARD FAIRS AT CENTRAL HALL, WESTMINSTER AND AT BRIGHTON. PLEASE WATCH OUR ADVERTISEMENTS FOR DETAILS OF THESE.

BLOOMSBURY CREST HOTEL
Coram Street · Russell Square · London WC1

Remaining dates for 1982:
September 19 · October 24 · November 28 · December 19

1983 Dates:
January 23 · February 20 · March 27 · April 24 · May 22 · June 26 · July 24
August 21 · October 2* · November 27 · December 18

* (This fair only will be held at **Regent Crest Hotel,** Carburton Street, London W1. (Next to P.O. Tower))

OPEN: 10 a.m. - 4.30 p.m.   ADMISSION 25p

Refreshments available   Nearest Tube: Russell Square

For further information or bookings:

IPM Promotions · 126 South Street · Dorking · Surrey RH4 2EU Tel: 0306 886008

62 Greyhound Hill, Hendon, London NW4.   **Tel: 01-203 1772**

163

Notes

Notes

INDEX

Headings in **bold** are chapters

ADVERTISERS' INDEX